Belfast City Hall, where Lord French took the Salute on 9th August, 1919.

THE GREAT WAR

1914-1918

ULSTER GREETS

HER BRAVE AND FAITHFUL SONS

AND REMEMBERS

HER GLORIOUS DEAD

 BooksUlster

First published in 1919. This new edition, with reset text published in 2015 by Books Ulster.

Typographical arrangement © Books Ulster.

Quotations from the works of Winston S. Churchill reproduced with permission of Curtis Brown, London on behalf of the Estate of Winston S. Churchill

ISBN: 978-1-910375-34-1

Contents

Foreword to the New Edition

In the centenary years of the Great War of 1914-1918 it is fitting that this book is republished. It not only provides a record of the actions and achievements of Ulstermen who served on the front, but also notes the efforts of non-combatants at home to support them. The horrors of that war can only be imagined, but not fully appreciated by today's generation. The conditions the men fought under, the torturous way in which so many died, and the deep and widescale grief of the bereaved is now beyond our true comprehension. However, it is right for us to continue to acknowledge their sacrifice and to understand that very little in war is glorious. Perhaps the greatest and most moving legacy of this account is in the reports of those soldiers who won distinction for selfless and humane action under threat of almost certain death. Their names and deeds deserve to be remembered.

Prefatory

This booklet does not profess to be in any sense an account of the manifold activities of the North of Ireland during the Great War. It is merely a few facts put together in souvenir form, which may be of interest to those who had the honour of participating in the historic events which are alluded to within these pages. If undue prominence appears to be given to the 36th Ulster Division, it must be remembered that alone of the divisions of the army it was composed of battalions of Ulster regiments from the beginning of the campaign until the end, and that a large percentage of the men who joined the army from the North of Ireland, especially from Belfast and district, served in the ranks of the Division. Equally gallant were the battalions of the Ulster regiments in the 10th and 16th Divisions and in the regular army. No distinction is made in the measure of praise that is due to Ulstermen of all creeds and classes who joined His Majesty's Forces in a period of great national emergency. The thanks of the committee in charge of the Peace celebrations, and the wider community which they represent, are tendered to one and all alike for their magnificent heroism which maintained the reputation not only of the Imperial Province of Ulster, but added imperishable renown to the name of Ireland.

August 9, 1919.

Greetings

VISCOUNT FRENCH, K.P., G.C.B., O.M., G.C.V.O.,
Lord Lieutenant of Ireland.

As the representative of His Majesty the King, I am to have the great honour of receiving the salute of the forces from Ulster who took part in the Great War, on the occasion of the Peace celebrations at Belfast.

I therefore wish to express my deep and heartfelt appreciation of the splendid services rendered by Ulstermen throughout the war and of their great deeds by land, sea, and air, in which they have so gloriously upheld the honour of Irish soldiers.

FRENCH,
VICEROY.

Greetings

ADMIRAL SIR DAVID BEATTY, G.C.B., G.C.V.O.
D.S.O.

On the occasion of the celebration of Peace I desire to record my appreciation of the part played by the men of Ulster, by sea, land and air, during the war.

In order that their sacrifices may not be thrown away and to ensure a lasting peace, it is necessary that they should continue to work together in the common cause and remain true to their traditions of loyalty.

David Beatty

Admiral of The Fleet

Greetings

FIELD-MARSHAL SIR DOUGLAS HAIG, K T.,
G.C.B., G.C.V.O., G.C.I.E.

I am glad to be given the opportunity to express to
the people of Ulster, now celebrating Peace, my high
appreciation of the many gallant deeds performed by
Ulstermen during the war.

I need but call to mind the opening attack of the Somme
battle in 1916, when men of the 36th Division, pressing
forward with the utmost courage and determination,
fought their way behind the defences of Thiepval to the
outskirts of Grandcourt. Or I might point to the capture
of the Messines Ridge in June, 1917, when Ulster men
drove the enemy from Wytschaete; to the clearing of
the west bank of the Canal du Nord in the Cambrai
operations in November, 1917; or to the great fight in
March of last year, on which occasion the 1st Battalion

Royal Inniskilling Fusiliers won undying fame.

These are but incidents in a long list of splendid actions which should be known to every Ulster man. I congratulate your men on the spirit they displayed in the great fight for the World's Liberty, and I hope that the Peace you are now celebrating will bring prosperity to Ulster, as to all parts of our Empire.

D. Haig.

The Great War

THE North of Ireland has no reason to be ashamed of the part it played in the Great War. Volumes could be written of the patriotic services of its sons and daughters during the four and a half years in which the British Empire was locked in deadly struggle with the Central Powers. Men and women of all creeds and classes laboured incessantly for the common cause, and whether duty called to the battlefield or to the high seas, or to the training camp or the munition shop, they had the satisfaction of knowing that their efforts had contributed to the overthrow of the Hun and the consumation of the victorious peace so enthusiastically celebrated in the capital of Ulster on 9th August 1919. Anything like a complete record of the activities of the people of the North is out of the question in the narrow confines of this little souvenir. Men, money, and munitions were freely given by the Imperial Province which it can fairly be claimed led the way in regard to all these matters.

The war loans were well supported in the North of Ireland, especially that of 1917, which provoked such a wave of practical patriotism that close on £40,000,000 was raised, of which the city of Belfast contributed £28,000,000. The 1919 loan was also heartily supported, not of course to the same extent as the efforts made during the war.

Between 4th February, 1914, and the 11th November, 1918, 75,000 men voluntarily enlisted in the army in the North of Ireland; no fewer than 46,000 of them were given by the City of Belfast. The 83rd Regimental District, comprising the Counties of Antrim and Down, including Belfast, had the highest return, the 27th Regimental area, comprising the Counties of Londonderry, Tyrone, Fermanagh, and Donegal being second, and the 87th Regimental area, comprising the Counties of Armagh, Monaghan, and Cavan, next. As a result of this response the normal establishment of the three Ulster regiments was enormously increased. The Royal Irish Rifles, which ordinarily possessed two regular and three special reserve battalions, had during the war in addition ten service battalions, four local reserve battalions, and one garrison battalion. The Royal Inniskilling Fusiliers, whose pre-war strength was two regular and two special reserve battalions, were increased by eight service battalions and one local reserve battalion, and the Royal Irish Fusiliers in place of two regular and two special reserve battalions were augmented by six service battalions, one local reserve battalion, and three garrison battalions. Not only did Ulster contribute largely to the two Irish Divisions, but it was the only province to raise a division entirely its own and provide the necessary reserve battalions for its maintenance on the field. The North of Ireland, which gave largely to the regular infantry, cavalry, and artillery, and in fact to every branch of the service, while many hundreds of men went to special units across the channel.

The activities of the Province did not end with sending the soldier into the field. Large sums were raised for the benefit of the men who were taken prisoners, for the comfort of men serving, for the providing of assistance for men broken in the wars and for the restoration to health of men wounded in the fight. The principal war philanthropies realised the following amounts:—

ULSTER OUR DAY COLLECTION

British Red Cross Society, Order of S. John of Jersualem.

1916	...	£27,735	1	8
1917	...	48,707	7	8
1918	...	70,137	2	2
Total	...	£146,579	1	6

Ulster Women's Gift Fund for Prisoners of War, etc.	£120,000
Ulster Patriotic Fund	100,000
Ulster Volunteer Force Hospitals, Belfast, Craigavon, and Gilford	100,000
Prince of Wales Fund	50,000
The Service Club, Belfast	20,000
Ulster Motor Ambulance Fund	12,000
Ulster Division Memorial Fund	5,000

Another branch of war work in which Ulster gave of its best was that in connection with hospitals. The U.V.F. Hospital in Botanic Avenue, which treated thousands of men, the Craigavon Hospital for neurasthenic cases, the Gilford Hospital, the Galwally Hospital, the Mental Hospital at Grosvenor Road, were creations of the war while the existing institutions, notably the Royal and the Mater in Belfast, the Infirmaries in Derry, Ballymena, Omagh, Downpatrick, and elsewhere placed many beds at the disposal of the authorities. All the time there was a vast stream of private beneficence going out towards those who were so' manfully upholding the honour of the Empire in the far-flung battle line. These are but a few of the war activities carried out here under while the men were fighting abroad. Mention might also be made of the Donegall Quay Buffet, and the buffets at the three railway termini in Belfast, at Portadown Station and elsewhere which refreshed hundreds of thousands of weary sailors and soldiers. And what of the Service Club in Belfast, which only closed its doors on 28th July last, but which will be talked of in every clime from shore to shore so long as there are survivors of the great war. During the twenty months of its existence it provided over 1,000,000 meals and 2,000,000 beds for men of the fighting forces. Equally useful was the work of the Rest House for Disabled Soldiers and Sailors in Castle Place, which provided refreshment, entertainment and rest for tens of thousands of soldiers in hospital blue, and the magnificent war service carried on in the city of Londonderry which assumed various forms.

The Graveyard of Ulster in France and Flanders is very large. It is largest around Thiepval, where the heroism of her sons is to be perpetuated by a noble memorial which will tell to all who pass by of the valour of the men from Ireland who died there in the great war. They are but a part, a small part of that mighty host which was swallowed up in the deadly struggle in France, in Gallipoli, in Servia, in Palestine, in Mesopotamia, in East Africa, on the high seas, and everywhere the Union Jack is raised aloft. They have died that others may live, yet they will speak to all generations through the imperishable memory they have bequeathed to Ulster, to Ireland, to the Empire, and to the world.

> On fame's eternal camping-ground
> Their silent tents are spread,
> And glory guards with solemn round
> The bivouac of the dead.

H.M. the King and Earl Kitchener at Ulster Division Review (Aldershot Command) on 30th September, 1915.

The 36th (Ulster) Division

THE 36th (Ulster) Division ranks as one of the most famous of the new army. Unique in the fact that it owed its origin to the period of grave domestic emergency that immediately preceded the war, the call to arms meant but the mobilisation of the flower of that force who had previously been brought together in the face of another crisis; its training was but the completion of that which had been begun long before the Hun broke loose; and its fighting produced a heroism unequalled by the legions of Marlborough or Wellington. The Division came into being as a unit of the New Army in the first week in September, when its Commander, Major-General C. H. Powell, C.B., and his staff, which included Lieut.-Col. Sir Jas. Craig, Bart., as A.A. and Q.M.G., arrived from England. Its original composition was:—

107TH BRIGADE.

(Brigadier-General G. H. H. Couchman, C.B.)

8th Battalion Royal Irish Rifles
(East Belfast Volunteers).
9th Battalion Royal Irish Rifles
(West Belfast Volunteers).
10th Battalion Royal Irish Rifles
(South Belfast Volunteers).
15th Battalion Royal Irish Rifles
(North Belfast Volunteers).

108TH BRIGADE.

(Brigadier-Gen. Sir G. Hacket Pain, K.B.E., C.B.)

11th Royal Irish Rifles
(South Antrim Volunteers).
12th Royal Irish Rifles
(Central Antrim Volunteers).
13th Royal Irish Rifles
(1st Co. Down Volunteers).
9th Royal Irish Fusiliers
(Armagh, Monaghan, and Cavan Volunteers).

109TH BRIGADE.

(Brigadier-Gen. T. E. Hickman, C.B., D.S.O.).

9th Royal Inniskilling Fusiliers
(Tyrone Volunteers).
10th Royal Inniskilling Fusiliers
(Derry Volunteers).
11th Royal Inniskilling Fusiliers
(Donegal and Fermanagh Volunteers).
14th Royal Irish Rifles
(Young Citizen Volunteers of Belfast).

PIONEER BATTALION

16th Battalion Royal Irish Rifles
(2nd Co. Down Volunteers).

DIVISIONAL TROOPS

Service Squadron, Inniskilling Dragoons.
153rd Brigade, Royal Field Artillery.

154th Brigade, Royal Field Artillery.
172nd Brigade, Royal Field Artillery.
173rd Brigade, Royal Field Artillery.
Divisional Ammunition Col., Royal Field Artillery.
121st Field Co., Royal Engineers.
122nd Field Co., Royal Engineers.
150th Field Co., Royal Engineers.
36th Divisional Signal Co., Royal Engineers.
Divisional Cyclists' Company.
108th Field Ambulance, R.A.M.C.
109th Field Ambulance, R.A.M.C.
110th Field Ambulance, R.A.M.C.
76th Sanitary Section, R.A.M.C.
Divisional Train, R.A.S.C.
48th Mobile Veterinary Section, R.A.V.C.
Army Chaplains' Dept.

(The artillery did not join the Division till it went to England. In 1915 six reserve battalions for draft finding purposes for the Division were formed, viz.: 17th, 18th, 19th, and 20th Royal Irish Rifles, 12th Royal Inniskilling Fusiliers, and 10th Royal Irish Fusiliers—the Division alone of the Irish Divisions having its own reserve formations.)

The first stages of the training of this imposing force were carried out at Ballykinlar, Clandeboye, Finner, Randalstown, and other camps in the North of Ireland. It was a strenuous time, every week adding to the impatience of the men to be up and doing. The pride of Ulster was thoroughly aroused by the only opportunity afforded the public of seeing it assembled as a whole. This was on the 8th May, 1915, when, with the exception of a battalion in quarantine, the entire Division was concentrated in Belfast for an inspection at Malone by Major-General Sir Hugh M'Calmont, K.C.B., followed by a march through the city, the salute being taken at the City Hall by the General. It was a memorable day, and the magnificent bearing of the troops won widespread admiration. The route was soon afterwards received, and June found the Division in the pleasant surroundings of Seaford, on the shores of the English Channel. A period of intensive training in the Aldershot command followed, in the course of which the Division was inspected by His Majesty the King, in the presence of the late Earl Kitchener and other distinguished soldiers. This notable event took place on 30th September, 1915, and subsequently the following gracious message from His Majesty was received:—

Officers, non-commissioned officers, and men, you are about to join your comrades at the front in bringing to a successful end this relentless war of over twelve months' duration.

Your prompt patriotic answer to the nation's call to arms will never be forgotten. The keen exertions of all ranks during the period of training have brought you to a state of efficiency not unworthy of my regular army.

I am confident that in the field you will nobly uphold the traditions of the fine regiments whose names you bear. Ever since your enrolment I have closely watched the growth and steady progress of all units. I shall continue to follow with interest the fortunes of your Division.

In bidding you farewell, I pray God may bless you in all your undertakings.

GEORGE, R.I.

IN FRANCE

Within a few days the Division was in France, having landed at Havre and Boulogne early in October. No time was lost dallying with the new attractions of foreign seaports. Men were required at the front, and very speedily the Ulsters heard the rumble of the guns in the Fonquivillers and Hebuterne sectors. The first soldier of the Division to fall in action was 19557 Rifleman Samuel Hill, 12th Royal Irish Rifles, son of Mr. Samuel Hill, Monkstown, Whiteabbey, who was a member of the Central Antrim U.V.F. He was killed on 22nd November, 1915. The first officer to lose his life was Sec.-Lieut. R. W. MacDermott, of the East Belfast Regiment, who was a son of Rev. Dr. MacDermott, Belmont.

At first the Division did not serve together. Various battalions were attached to divisions already in the line, as will be seen from the brief official histories which appear later on. By February, 1916, the brigades were all together, and Major-General Nugent, C.B., D.S.O., a distinguished Ulsterman, who had succeeded Major-General Powell before the Division came overseas, thereafter had his magnificent force directly under his command in the Thiepval area. The winter was a trying one, raids and bombardments being the daily accompaniments of the hardships of trench life. June, 1916, was spent in preparation for the great push which everyone knew was coming.

THIEPVAL

The Division went over the top for the first time on the morning of 1st July, 1916, which witnessed the beginning of the prolonged Battle of the Somme. It made its name on that memorable yet bloody day, when it carried five lines of trenches with irresistible dash; but for want of support they had to be given up, and the sun went down with thousands of dead and wounded Ulstermen on the slopes of Thiepval. Countless deeds of heroism were performed on that day, which brought the Division four Victoria Crosses and many other decorations. The story of the attack need not be repeated. It is known to all Ulstermen. Colonel John Buchan's History of the War records that

North of Thiepval the Ulster Division broke through the enemy trenches, passed the crest of the ridge, and reached the point called The Crucifix, in rear of the first German position. For a little they held the strong Schwaben Redoubt, which we were not to enter again till after three months of battle, and some even got into the outskirts of Grandcourt. It was the anniversary day of the Battle of the Boyne, and that charge, when the men shouted, "Remember the Boyne!" will be for ever a glorious page in the annals of Ireland. Enfiladed on three sides, they went on through successive German lines, and only a remnant came back to tell the tale. That remnant brought many prisoners, one man herding fifteen of the enemy through their own barrage. In the words of the General who commanded it: "The Division carried out every portion of its allotted task in spite of the heaviest losses. It captured nearly 600 prisoners, and carried its advance triumphantly to the limits of the objective laid down." Nothing finer was done in the war. The splendid troops drawn from those Volunteers who had banded themselves together for another cause now shed their blood like water for the liberty of the world.

The casualties ran into thousands, and included close on 250 officers. The officer losses were so severe that some battalions had practically none left at the close of the day. They were made up as follows:—8th Royal Irish Rifles, officers killed, wounded, and missing, 20; 9th Royal Irish Rifles, 20; 10th Royal Irish Rifles, 18; 11th Royal Irish Rifles, 14; 12th Royal Irish Rifles, 17; 13th Royal Irish Rifles, 18; 14th Royal Irish Rifles, 16; 15th Royal Irish Rifles, 15; 9th Royal Irish Fusiliers, 18; 9th Royal Inniskilling Fusiliers, 16; 10th Royal Inniskilling Fusiliers, 12; 11th Royal Inniskilling Fusiliers, 15; 16th R. I. Rifles, 1; Machine Gun Cos., 8; Trench Mortar Batteries, 9. The province of Ulster was thrown into mourning by the awful death roll. Several families lost two and three sons. Amongst those who fell were the gallant Colonel

H. C. Bernard, of the South Belfast Volunteers; Major
G. H. Gaffikin, of the West Belfast Volunteers, who led
his men on waving an orange handkerchief; Capt. J. S.
Davidson, of the Sirocco Works, most fearless of machine
gunners; Capt. P. Cruickshank, a popular journalist of
the Tyrones; Capt. J. C. B. Proctor, of Limavady; Major A.
Uprichard, Capt. W. H. Smyth, and Lieut. G. A. Rogers,
three heroic West Down sportsmen; Capt. E. Johnston, of
Newtownards; Capt. C. O. Slacke, of Wheatfield, Belfast;
Capt. Douglas O'Flaherty, and Lieut. Victor Robb, the
ardent city motorists; Capt. Bertie Tate, and Capt. W. H.
Chiplin, the Church Lads' Brigade enthusiast; Capt. C.
F. K. Ewart, Capt. O. B. Webb, Capt. C. S. Murray, Lieut.
E. Vance, Lieut. A. D. Lemon, Lieut. W. M'Cluggage,
Lieut. R. H. Neill, Lieut. T. G. Haughton, Lieut. L. B.
Campbell, Lieut. Sir E. H. Macnaghten, Bart., all well-
known Co. Antrim men; Lieut. G. St. G. S. Cather, the
Adjutant of the Armaghs, who won the V.C. on that day;
the two officer sons of Mr. J. H. Hewitt, of Bangor, of
the late Mr. Jas. Hollywood, J.P., Belfast, and of the late
Rev. G. R. Wedgwood, of Belfast. The prisoners taken
included Capt. C. C. Craig, M.P. for South Antrim, who
remained in the hands of the Germans for many long
weary months afterwards.

A distinguished English staff officer, writing to
Lieutenant-Colonel Fred Crawford, Belfast, on 3rd July,
said:—

The Division has been through an ordeal by fire,
gas, and poison. It has behaved marvellously, and has

got through all the German lines.

Our gallant fellows marched into a narrow alley of death, shouting "No Surrender!" and "Remember the Boyne!"

I wish I had been born an Ulsterman, but I am proud to have been associated with these wonderful men—the most gallant in the world. I fully realise how you feel where you are.

Many a family in Ulster will have lost a son or a father out here. I do not believe men ever passed to another world in so glorious a light.

After the day before yesterday I hope I may be allowed the rest of my life to maintain my association with the Ulster Province.

The following is a copy of the celebrated order of the day issued after the battle:—

SPECIAL ORDER OF THE DAY

By Major-General O. S. W. Nugent, D.S.O., Commanding 36th (Ulster) Division.

The General Officer Commanding the Ulster Division desires that the Division should know that, in his opinion, nothing finer has been done in the war than the attack by the Ulster Division on the 1st July.

The leading of the Company Officers, the discipline and courage shown by all ranks of the Division will stand out in the future history of the war as an example of what good troops, well led, are capable of accomplishing.

None but troops of the best quality could have faced the fire which was brought to bear on them and the losses suffered during the advance.

Nothing could have been finer than the steadiness and discipline shown by every battalion, not only in forming up outside its own trenches, but in advancing under severe enfilading fire.

The advance across the open to the German line was carried out with the steadiness of a parade movement, under a fire both from front and flanks, which could only have been faced by troops of the highest quality.

The fact that the objects of the attack on one side were not obtained is no reflection on the battalions which were entrusted with the task.

They did all that man could do, and in common with every battalion in the Division, showed the most conspicuous courage and devotion.

On the other side, the Division carried out every portion of its allotted task in spite of the heaviest losses.

It captured nearly 600 prisoners, and carried its advance triumphantly to the limits of the objective laid down.

There is nothing in the operations carried out by the Ulster Division on the 1st July that will not be a source of pride to all Ulstermen.

The Division has been highly tried, and has emerged from the ordeal with unstained honour, having fulfilled, in every particular, the great expectations formed of it.

Tales of individual and collective heroism on the part of officers and men come in from every side, too numerous to mention, but all showing that the standard of gallantry and devotion attained is one that may be equalled, but is never likely to be surpassed.

The General Officer Commanding deeply regrets the heavy losses of officers and men. He is proud beyond description, as every officer and man in the Division may well be, of the magnificent example of sublime courage and discipline which the Ulster Division has given to the Army.

Ulster has every reason to be proud of the men she has given to the service of our country.

Though many of our best men have gone, the spirit which animated them remains in the Division, and will never die.

L. J. COMYN,
Lt.-Col., A.A. and Q.M.G.,
36th Division.

3rd July, 1916.

Thiepval on the eve of the Great Attack on 1st July, 1916

Messines and Ypres

Withdrawn from the Somme area to make good its terrible losses, the replacing of which depleted the reserve battalions at home, the Division was transferred to the Second Army in Flanders, under General Plumer. It spent the remainder of 1916 in the Ploegsteert, Messines, and neighbouring areas, where it enhanced its already illustrious name by successful raiding. The spring and early summer of 1917 saw the Ulsters still in the northern area, and on 7th June it took part, side by side with the 16th Irish Division, in that brilliant offensive which gave the British possession of the Wytscharte-Messines Ridge, which had been 2½ years in the hands of the enemy. In this great attack the Division was conspicuously successful, securing the third German line at a cost of 170 killed and 900 wounded. The "Times'" correspondent recorded that the Ulster Division did its work cleanly and beautifully, and General Sir Hubert Gough, K.C.B., wrote:—

In this battle the Ulster Division displayed the greatest courage and dash, as well as the greatest discipline and training.

Their conduct was splendid, and I am happy to say the results were as splendid as the conduct which led to them.

Amongst those who fell on the day of victory were:— Major F. W. L. May, a well-known Belfast Rugby footballer;

Captain H. Gallaugher, D.S.O., of Manorcunningham, who had displayed great gallantry at Thiepval; Captain Arthur K. M'Bride, of the firm of H. J. M'Bride & Son, Ltd., Hydepark; Lieutenant Robert M'Laurin, of South Belfast Volunteers; Second-Lieutenants Brian Boyd and S. J. L. Downey, of the Y.C.V.'s, and W. S. Ferris, son of the late Rev. James C. Ferris, of Windsor Presbyterian Church, Belfast. The East Belfast Regiment had the heaviest losses of the day, 170 of all ranks being killed, wounded, and missing. Many decorations were awarded for this battle.

A brief period of rest, and the Division went into the line again, north-east of Ypres, in the first week of August, when a terrible fortnight ended in the attack at Frezenberg on 16th August, which called forth the highest courage. The ground was a swamp, the weather was atrocious, and through a morass of shell-holes, in which wounded men were drowned, the attack was pressed home; but in the process various units, notably the 9th Battalion Royal Irish Fusiliers, were all but annihilated. This long and desperate fight was like a nightmare. In some respects, says Col. Buchan, the histories have no parallel for colossal difficulty and naked misery among the shell-holes and tortured ridges of the Ypres salient. It was a soldiers' battle, like the spring and summer fighting of 1915, and as such was made conspicuous by gallant deeds. The Belfast Brigade, which went in on 2nd August, had an awful time in the trenches, losing many officers and men, including Major G. E. M'Coll, of the 8th Royal Irish Rifles. Frezenberg was only the culmination of this terrible fortnight. The Ulsters were up against the most obstinate part of the line.

The difficulty of making deep-mined dug-outs in soil where water lay within a few feet of the surface of the ground had compelled the enemy to construct in the ruins of farms and other suitable localities a number of strong points or "pill-boxes" built of reinforced concrete often many feet thick. These field forts, distributed in depth all along the front of our advance, offered a serious obstacle to progress. They were heavily armed with machine guns and manned by men determined to hold on at all costs. Many were reduced as our troops advanced. In addition, weather conditions made aeroplane observation practically impossible, with the result that no warning was received of the enemy's counter-attacks, and our infantry obtained little artillery help against them.

Philip Gibbs describes how the Germans swept the entire line from Hill 35, a spur reaching out from the Zonnebeke Road across the centre of the battlefield, and dominating all the approaches from the trenches of the North of Ireland men. The Volunteers were raked from many enemy strong posts, particularly at Pond Farm, the scene of a terrific struggle, and Gallipoli Fort, while the difficulty of the task entrusted to them was accentuated by the bad state of the ground. The Ulstermen occupied Hill 35 for a time, but were forced off it. "Then the counter-attacks drove in the thinned but still determined line of Irishmen, and they came back across the riddled ground, some of them wounded, all in the last stages of exhaustion, pausing in their unwilling journey to fire at the snipers who harassed them, and reaching at last the trenches they left at dawn, angry and bitter and disappointed, but undismayed—the heroes of a splendid failure."

The losses included Lt.-Col. A. C. Pratt, of the Donegals; Lt.-Col. S. J. Somerville, of the Armaghs, and his gallant Transport officer, Lieut. J. M. Stronge, only son of Sir Jas. Stronge, Bart., of Tynan; Capt. H. D. Eccles, the medical officer of the Co. Downs, and many subalterns of the Y.C.V.'s and other battalions; whilst the wounded included Lt.-Col. R. D. Perceval Maxwell, of Finnebrogue. The 9th Royal Irish Fusiliers had 21 officer casualties on 16th August alone. After this ordeal, the Division was taken out of the line to reorganise.

Cambrai and St. Quentin

THE southern zone (Third Army) was the next destination of the Ulster Division, which, owing to the heavy losses it had been sustaining, was constantly changing its personnel, drafts from home being quickly swallowed up. Leaving the Ypres salient in August, the intervening period was spent in reserve and in the trenches south-west of Cambrai. The 8th and 9th Rifles were amalgamated in September, as were the 11th and 13th Rifles. The 1st Battalion Royal Irish Fusiliers (regulars) were brought into the 107th Brigade, and the 2nd Battalion Royal Irish Rifles to the 108th Brigade, in which the 9th Battalion Royal Irish Fusiliers received a draft of 500 men of the North Irish Horse. September and October were spent in the trenches in the Hermies sector; but the next great operation in which the Division was involved was the attack on the Hindenburg line, which began on 20th November. Sir A. Conan Doyle makes eulogistic reference to the part played by the Division in this struggle, which did not achieve its main object owing to fog. He says:—

The British front was cut across diagonally by a considerable canal with deep sides—the Canal du Nord. Upon the north side of this was one division. This flank unit was the famous 36th Ulsters, who behaved this day with their usual magnificent gallantry. Advancing with deliberate determination, they carried all before them, though exposed to that extra strain to which a flank unit must always submit. Their left was enfiladed by the enemy, and they had continually to build up a defensive line which naturally subtracted from their numbers and made a long advance impossible. None the less, after rushing a high bank bristling with machine-guns, they secured the second Hindenburg line, where they were firmly established by 10-30, after a sharp contest with the garrison. They then swept forward, keeping the canal upon their right, until by evening they had established themselves upon the Bapaume-Cambrai road.

The Division gained its objectives on 20th and 21st, and held on against counter-attacks on the 22nd. The 107th Brigade was in reserve at first. It was soon employed to develop the successes gained. The 8/9th Rifles distinguished themselves on 23rd by capturing Round Trench and Quarry Wood, near Mouvres. The battalion was isolated, and had to evacuate the wood, but it stuck to Round Trench till relieved. The engineers of the Division displayed wonderful heroism in these Cambrai operations, which cost the Division many valuable lives, including some officers who could ill be spared, notably Capt. W. B. G. Stuart, of Ballymena; Capt. D. M'Causland, of St. Johnston, and Capt. J. C. Jamison, of Belfast. Lieut. Geo. York Henderson, son of the late Sir James Henderson, of Belfast, also fell, as did Lieuts. T. S. Haslett and J. Smyth, both of Ballymena, and a considerable number of second-lieutenants, N.C.O.'s and men. Following the great battle, the Division fought in various encounters on the Hindenburg line, in the vicinity of Havrincourt Wood.

One very fierce struggle took place at La Vacquerie in the first week of December, which cost the Tyrones five officers killed and many men. One of the officers who lost his life at this place, the late Second-Lieut. J. S. Emerson, was posthumously awarded the Victoria Cross, the fifth for the Division. In January, 1918, the Ulsters moved further S.E. to relieve the French in the St. Quentin sector.

Early in 1918 the reorganisation of the Army into brigades of three battalions led to further changes. The 8/9th Rifles were disbanded in February, as were the 10th, 11/13th and 14th Rifles, and the 10th and 11th Royal Inniskilling Fusiliers, the personnel of each being drafted into other battalions of their own regiments. The composition of the infantry brigades just before a very eventful period in their history, the retreat of March, was as follows:—

107TH BRIGADE.
1st Battalion Royal Irish Rifles.
2nd Battalion Royal Irish Rifles.
15th Battalion Royal Irish Rifles.

108TH BRIGADE.
12th Battalion Royal Irish Rifles.
1st Battalion Royal Irish Fusiliers.
9th Battalion Royal Irish Fusiliers.

109TH BRIGADE.
1st Battalion Royal Inniskilling Fusiliers.
2nd Battalion Royal Inniskilling Fusiliers.
9th Battalion Royal Inniskilling Fusiliers.

It will thus be seen that all the regular battalions of the Ulster regiments, save the 2nd Battalion Royal Irish Fusiliers, which was in the East, had now been brought into the Division which was about to undergo a fiery ordeal. It was then part of the XVIII. Corps, commanded by Lieut.-Gen. Sir Ivor Maxse. The story of the arduous operations, which commenced on 21st March near St. Quentin, and ended on the River Avre, near Moreuil, is briefly as follows:—

On the 21st March, in a dense mist, three battalions of the Division held a front of 6,000 yards in the Forward Zone, and also occupied ground to a depth of some 1,200 yards from their outposts. These heroic battalions were first subjected to an intensive bombardment by all calibres of guns and trench mortars for a period of five hours, and were then overwhelmed by not less than three German infantry divisions. Little remains of the three battalions, but we have evidence of their heroism from some men of the 12th Royal Irish Rifles, who swam down the canal at night and reported that their battalion was still holding out in the Racecourse Redoubt after 24 hours incessant fighting. Their gallantry will live for ever in the annals of their regiments, and they undoubtedly accounted for great numbers of the enemy.

After our Forward Zone had thus been overwhelmed,

the enemy continuously assaulted our Battle Zone, and suffered casualties in spite of the continuance of the mist which deprived our gunners and machine gunners of targets. At only one point, Contescourt, did he gain a footing on the divisional front on 21st March, and the Battle Zone would probably have remained intact in our hands if its right had not been completely turned at Essigny, in an adjoining area. The loss of Essigny and the consequent necessity of immediately forming a deep flank to our right used up in the reserves of the 36th Division which had been allotted for counter-attacks in the Battle Zone. The Redoubt at Fontaine-les-Clercs, so gallantly held by the 1st Battalion Royal Inniskilling Fusiliers, repulsed no less than twelve desperate attacks, and would have been saved by counter-attacks if the reserve battalion had been available in its brigade. But it could not be in two places at once, and thus a breach unavoidable occurred in the Battle Zone on 22nd March.

The result of the two days' fighting was that its Battle Zone had to be vacated by the 36th Division in order to safeguard the right flank of the Corps, and this was accomplished after casualties had again been inflicted on the assaulting enemy. The withdrawal took place during the evening and night of 22nd March.

The subsequent retreat was conducted in good order, and involved daily rearguard actions along the whole front. During these actions the 121st Field Company R.E., at St. Simon, and the other companies R.E. elsewhere, performed admirable services under fire, and destroyed 27 bridges. The 9th Battalion Royal Irish Fusiliers charged with the Royal Dragoons at Villeselves. Forty machine-gunners recaptured Erches and accounted for 200 of the enemy. The 109th Infantry Brigade held Guerbigny long after it was isolated on 27th March.

The Divisional Artillery, as also the 179th Brigade of Army Field Artillery and the 35th Heavy Artillery Brigade, all performed most excellent services throughout the operations, the 179th Brigade being especially well handled in the early stages of the battle. Moreover, the French generals under whom our artillery served during the past critical days of these operations have expressed grateful appreciation of the valuable support given by all the above-mentioned artillery to the French infantry.

The losses in the retreat were over 5,000, of whom the vast majority were taken prisoners, having been cut off by the advancing Germans. The number of killed was much less than at Thiepval, but it was substantial. Amongst the officers who fell were Capt. H. M. Bailie, Belfast, and Capt. W. H. Madden (Campbell College), both of the Pioneer Battalion; Capt. J. F. Harvey, of Downshire Road, Cregagh; Capt. G. W. Vesey, of Derrabard, Co. Tyrone; Lieut. T. L. M'Cay, Castlederg; Lieut. Jas. Kerr, of Belfast; Lieut. W. D. Magookin, 12th Rifles, formerly of York Street Mill, who was the first N.C.O. to win a decoration in the Division, having been awarded the D.C.M. when serving in the 15th (North Belfast) Battalion in 1915, on the occasion that Sec.-Lieut. H. de la M. Harpur, of the same battalion, won the first Military Cross gained by the Ulsters; Second-Lieuts. Jas. Kennedy, J. C. Thompson, E. E. Burnside, R. V. Lyons, all of Belfast; A. O. Houston

(Maghera), R. W. Gilmour (Coleraine), T. L. Clements (Omagh). Another officer who fell was Second-Lieut. Edmund De Wind, 15th Royal Irish Rifles, of Comber, one of the Division's V.C.'s. The other St. Quentin V.C., Second-Lieut. C. L. Knox, of the 150th Field Co. R.E., survived the retreat. The prisoners included Lieut.-Col. Lord Farnham, commanding the 2nd Inniskillings, and Lt.-Col. C. O. Place, of the Headquarters' Staff.

MESSINES AND BAILLEUL, 1918
IN THE FURNACE AGAIN

The shattered Division was fairly entitled to a rest, so "Northward Ho!" was the order. Refitting was carried out in marvellously short time at Cassel, and in a few days the 36th were holding the Passchendaele trenches. But the 108th Brigade had a terrible experience. Marching to join the other brigades, it was suddenly called on to stem the desperate German thrust for the Channel ports. The fighting was of the most intense nature, and the brigade, fresh from the fire of St. Quentin into the furnace at Messines, lost many officers and men, of whom none were better known than Lieut.-Col. Blair Oliphant, D.S.O., Lisburn; Major Holt Waring, of Waringstown; Capt. T. E. Crosbie, M.C., of Portadown, and Capt. C. B. Despard, D.S.O., M.C., Belfast. It was but a remnant of General Griffith's Brigade that survived to join the other brigades towards the end of April, where it spent the next three months in the vicinity of Mont des Cats. Early in May General Nugent relinquished command, and was succeeded by General Clifford Coffin, V.C., who had greatly distinguished himself right through the war. He had a stiff task of reorganisation after the losses, and seeing that many of the drafts that came to him were mere lads, the subsequent history of the Division contains some of its brightest pages. The enemy was lively during the summer, and there were many casualties, chiefly from gas. The German attack long threatened never came, and the offensive emanating from the British side, thereafter the initiative passed for ever from the Boche.

The culminating point in this sector held by the 36th Division was reached when, after a brilliant attack on 24th August carried out by the 1st and 9th Battalions Royal Irish Fusiliers and the 15th Royal Irish Rifles, in which the whole of the German system of trenches defending Bailleul was carried on the front of over a mile, the enemy retired eastwards on a wide front, evacuating Kemmel Hill and Bailleul. The Division was not slow in exploiting this success; the 109th Brigade had come into the line and taken over the new positions captured by the 107th and 108th Brigades on the night of 24th August. The German withdrawal was immediately observed by them, and on the morning of 26th August the whole of the Division was advancing in pursuit.

The change from three months' almost continuous trench warfare to mobile fighting in the open was a sudden one. To change instantly from warfare of this nature and advance in pursuit of an enemy whose position and intentions are unknown is one of the most difficult operations in war, yet the Ulster Division accomplished it with conspicuous success inside 24 hours. The Inniskilling Brigade kept in touch with the enemy and drove him across the famous Ravelsberg Ridge at one bound, and fought him like tigers until his next main position of defence at Neuve Eglise was reached. Their casualties were heavy, as the Boches defence was stubborn, and the 2nd Battalion had the misfortune to lose their gallant commander, Lieutenant-Colonel Knott, D.S.O., who was badly wounded on 30th August, but they stuck to their work until relieved by the 108th Brigade.

This sector of the front was very familiar to such of the officers and men as had served with the Division in the months preceding the assault on the Messines Ridge in June, 1917. Bailleul, now a heap of ruins in the hands of the enemy, was at that time a veritable Mecca, within easy reach of Divisional Headquarters at Dranoutre. It was on the main road from Messines to Bailleul that the Division had now to experience severe fighting in the capture of Neuve Eglise. The 109th Brigade, after the hard work they had had from 26th to 31st August, had halted and dug a rough line of trenches in touch with the enemy in this position, when orders were received that the 108th Brigade would advance through them and attack Neuve Eglise and Wulverghem on the morning of 1st September.

The night of 31st August was moonlight, and the 1st Royal Irish Fusiliers and 12th Royal Irish Rifles advanced in artillery formations north and south of the main road respectively, reaching the outskirts of Neuve Eglise as dawn was breaking, with the 9th Royal Irish Fusiliers in support on the Ravelsberg Ridge. The enemy settled down to a stubborn defence of the village from excellent positions, sweeping the main street with a fire so intense that all progress was stopped. Such, however, was the splendid initiative displayed by company and platoon commanders that the advance was continued both north and south of the village, and by 10 a.m. on the morning of 1st September Neuve Eglise was almost surrounded, although the German machine-gunners concealed there, continued to occupy their emplacements, and both battalions suffered heavily from a heavy fire on their flanks.

The situation was serious; further progress could not be made until the village was captured, and enemy guns which had hitherto been silent commenced a heavy and accurate bombardment of our positions, increasing the casualties to an alarming extent. Something had to be done, and to be done quickly, so Lieutenant-Colonel G. Thomson, of Larne, commanding the 12th Royal Irish Rifles, detailed a company, under his adjutant, Captain W. J. Lyness, M.C., of Tullyard, Moira, to make a direct attack on the village under covering fire from Stokes' mortars. This attack, in the face of a terrific enemy fire, succeeded, and by 4 p.m. in the afternoon the village was in our hands. As an example of dashing advanced guard action this operation was well carried out, as the enemy position was one in which he had certainly intended to stay for several days.

At 9 o'clock next morning the advance was continued south of Wulverghem, which fell into our hands. Nearing the ridge, a violent enemy bombardment soon made it clear that it was not to be a walk-over, and enemy machine-guns concealed in excellent positions in the Lys valley began to disclose themselves. A halt was made until the situation was reconnoitred, and on the night of the 2nd the 9th Royal Irish Fusiliers took over the whole line preparatory to a fresh attack at dawn the following day. But during that night German reinforcements came pouring up to the line, and when the Fusiliers attacked on the morning of the 3rd the resistance was of a very stiff nature, and although Hill 63 was captured and held against determined counter-attacks, little further progress could be made.

The 107th Brigade took over the line on the 6th September, and made attack after attack to gain the Messines Ridge, but it was now proved beyond dispute that to push the enemy further would be impossible unless large forces were employed. The 107th Brigade stuck to the ground won, however, with determination and stubbornness, although the shell fire had now increased to an appalling density, and their casualties were heavy. The 2nd Royal Irish Rifles lost their commander, Lieutenant-Colonel J. H. Bridcutt, D.S.O., killed, and the 15th Royal Irish Rifles had the misfortune to lose Lieut.-Colonel R. C. Smythe, D.S.O., wounded, in addition to many other officers. Shortly afterwards, too, the 2nd Royal Inniskilling Fusiliers had the misfortune to lose Lieutenant-Colonel L. de V. Fitzgerald, killed, and Major G. M. Forde, D.S.O., M C., wounded.

FLANDERS
WITH THE BELGIAN ARMY

Subsequent operations in this region were carried out by other troops, and the Ulster Division received orders a few days later to proceed north, where, in conjunction with the 9th and 29th Divisions forming the Second Corps, it was to cooperate with the Belgian Army in what proved to be the final offensive. This phase of the operations began on 28th September near Ypres, when the Ulsters were in support. The Germans retired so rapidly at first that the troops in reserve had to march hard to keep up with the attacking divisions. The Germans eventually put their backs to the wall, as it were, in the hills around the village of Becelaire.

On the morning of the 29th, therefore, the 'Skins Brigade came into action, the 1st and 2nd battalions attacking the village and the high ground on either side. This attack was a complete success and very gallantly carried out, and the enemy fell back upon his next position, a similar line of hills on the east of Dadazeele. The 2nd Inniskillings pushed on and occupied Dadazeele, about two miles further than their prescribed objective, taking the enemy completely by surprise, and capturing prisoners, and what was equally important, bringing the fighting into territory hitherto little scarred by the ravages of war.

The Germans stuck to Hill 41, east of Dadazeele, which gave a fine view away towards Courtrai. The 108th Brigade was ordered to take the hill, which was attacked with great heroism, but which cost us many valuable lives, including Capt. W. C. Boomer, M.C., of the 12th Rifles, a Lisburn officer, and Capt. A. P. I. Samuels, of the N. West Bar. Fighting was renewed on the morning of 1st October, when the 1st Royal Irish Fusiliers succeeded in gaining the crest of the hill, capturing several stubbornly-defended positions, but only to find innumerable fresh enemy nests of machine-guns disputing their advance. Progress was impossible, and casualties were so high that the battalion seemed to wither away. A line of shallow trenches, however, was dug on the very crest of the hill, and held against a German counter-attack, which developed without success in the forenoon of 1st October.

The 107th Brigade attack further south had also met with a terrific resistance, and the Rifle battalions had been stopped with heavy casualties. Reinforcements were not forthcoming, and when the enemy opened a heavy counter-attack against the 12th Royal Irish Rifles and the 1st Royal Irish Fusiliers in the afternoon, the situation became a serious one. But the two battalions had no intention of giving up what they had won, and the survivors, tired and worn out as they were, settled down to a defence which for sheer hard fighting had few equals in the war. All the ground was held till it was time to go ahead again.

The rapidity of the advance had left the heavy guns far in the rear, and it was decided to wait till they came up. The intervening period, October 2nd-14th, was a trying one, and the Germans shelled the trenches frequently, while there were numerous local attacks by each side.

The losses of this period included Lieut.-Col. P. E. Kelly, the gallant young C.O. of the 9th Royal Irish Fusiliers, who was killed on 10th October, and Capt. G. J. Bruce, D.S.O., M.C., the Comber cricketer, who was Brigade-Major of the 109th Brigade.

The offensive was resumed, and after a heavy bombardment, the Inniskilling Brigade dashed to the fray and took Hill 41. The Germans fled, and next day the Division was in the north-east part of Courtrai, being the first troops to enter. The enemy, however, blew up the principal bridge over the Lys Canal communicating with the main part of the city. The Engineers pontooned it under heavy fire, but before the infantry crossed the Division was relieved. It went north immediately, and crossed the Lys at Oyghem in face of severe fire, the 109th Brigade and the Engineers earning great credit for their work. The Germans were forced steadily back to the Scheldt. In the fighting that began on 14th October and lasted till the Division was relieved there were many casualties. Lieut.-Col. B. J. Jones, D.S.O., of the 15th Royal Irish Rifles, was mortally wounded, and others who fell were Capt. G. B. J. Smyth, of Banbridge; Capt. C. E. Walkington, of Belfast; Capt. H. G. Morrow, M.C., of Belfast; Capt. M. H. Gibson, M.C., of Belfast; and Lieut. E. Daniel, of Dungannon. Two Victoria Crosses were awarded for the Flanders fighting, both going to the Inniskillings.

On 27th the Division was taken out for a rest. But its fighting was done. The armistice came before the Division had been refitted after its three months of heavy fighting, and thereafter it quartered in the town of Mouscron, whence most of the men went home to demobilise.

H.R.H. the Prince of Wales paid a special visit to the Ulster Division from 30th January to 1st February, 1919, inclusive, on his return journey from Germany. The visit was of an informal nature, no reviews or inspections being held, but the Prince was able to see and converse with the officers and men of every battalion in the Division, despite the inclement weather and the dispersed billets. Royal Inniskilling Fusiliers, Royal Irish Rifles, Royal Irish Fusiliers, and most of the Divisional Troops (including the sick in Field Ambulances) were visited in turn, the Prince being received everywhere with much enthusiasm.

The cadres of the regular battalions returned to England in the spring, and those of the service battalions (save the 12th Rifles) in June, reaching their respective depots at Belfast, Omagh, and Armagh on the 15th of the month. They had a good reception, but it would have been more elaborate had the authorities given earlier notice of the arrival of the troops. The 12th Battalion was retained for service with the Army of Occupation, and having been brought up to strength by volunteers from other units, was sent to the Rhine, where it is still quartered.

MARSHAL FOCH'S THANKS

The following orders are of interest:—

22nd October, 1918.

36th Division.

Marshal Foch visited the Army Commander to-day and asked him to send his congratulations to the II. Corps and to the 9th, 29th, and 36th Divisions for their splendid work in the operations since the 14th October. Please communicate the above to all ranks. The Divisional Commander congratulates all ranks on the splendid fighting qualities exhibited by them which have won this approbation from Marshal Foch. (Signed),

A. G. THOMSON,

Lieut.-Colonel, G.S.,

36th (Ulster) Division.

22/10/18.

The Corps Commander issued the following order relative to the closing Flanders operations:—

The 36th (Ulster Division) has been fighting continuously since the 28th September in the operations in Flanders. The spirit, dash, and initiative shown by all ranks have been splendid and beyond all praise. The leadership displayed by yourself and your brigade and other commanders could not have been better. The conditions under which the men have had to fight have been trying, but nothing seemed to stop your gallant Division.

I have also been struck with the good staff work of the Division, and it is very creditable to all concerned.

Will you kindly express to the commanders, staffs, and all ranks of the Division my heartiest congratulations and thanks for their work?

When the history is written of what the Division has done in Flanders during the past month it will prove to be a record of magnificent fighting and a wonderful progress, for during this period an advance has been made of about twenty-five miles over the worst of country and under the heaviest machine-gun fire ever experienced in this war. This advance has entailed constant fighting, but the 36th Division has overcome every obstacle and has proved itself to be one of the best fighting divisions in the army—well commanded and well staffed.

My best wishes to you all.

OFFICIAL HISTORIES

Appended will be found official statements of the service of several of the battalions of the Division, issued by the Adjutant-General of the Forces. One is chosen from each brigade:—

8TH ROYAL IRISH RIFLES—107TH BRIGADE.

The battalion was formed in 1914, and, after undergoing training in England, left Bramshott on October 3rd, 1915, landing at Boulogne next day. It was attached to the 12th Brigade for instruction in the Mailly Maillet area, and later to the 10th Brigade.

In November the whole 107th Brigade was transferred to the Fourth Division, with which the battalion continued for three months, serving in the section north of Ancre.

In February, 1916, the 107th Brigade rejoined the Ulster Division, and served with it in the Mailly Maillet and Thiepval areas till the offensive of July 1, when it took part in the attack on Thiepval. The battalion was successful in gaining its third objective, but could go no further, though it held on until relieved on July 3, despite several counter-attacks.

The Division was then transferred to Belgium, and the battalion was in the line at Ploegsteert and in neighbouring sectors through the winter of 1916-1917 and until April, 1917, when it was taken out for an extended period of training. The chief incident of this period was the repulse on March 24 of a hostile raid.

On June 7 the battalion took a prominent part in the successful attack on the Messines Ridge; it captured both its objectives near L'Enfer Wood, and, though it had 170 casualties, was most successful, receiving four M.C's, a D.C.M., and eight M.M's.

In July the battalion was out in Army Reserve, and was put into the line East of Ypres on August 2nd; here it had heavy fighting, and lost heavily, though only in support in the attack of August 16. It then moved to the Third Army, and was in reserve near Etrincourt, when, on August 28, it was amalgamated with the 9th Battalion Royal Irish Rifles, and redesignated the 8/9th Battalion Royal Irish Rifles.

The amalgamated battalion remained in this area (Havrincourt) till the great attack on the Hindenburg line in November. In this it was put in on November 23 against Round Trench and Quarry Wood, near Mouvres.

It took both of these, but, being isolated, had to evacuate the wood, though it maintained its hold on Round Trench till relieved.

Subsequently the amalgamated battalion was in trenches at Lechelle (December) and near Bonchy (January, 1918), and on being disbanded (February 6), the personnel of the battalion was divided between the 1st, 2nd (Regular), 12th, and 15th (Service) Battalions.

In every engagement in which this battalion took part it upheld the brilliant and glorious traditions of the Royal Irish Rifles to which it belonged.

Battalions of this regiment have served in all quarters of the globe, and have taken part in such historic battles as—Cape of Good Hope, Talavera, Bourbon, Busaco, Fuentes d'Onor, Ciudad Rodrigo, Badajoz, Salamanca, Vittoria, Nivelle, Orthes, Toulouse, Peninsula, and in the campaigns in India, Central India, and South Africa, 1899-1902.

Although the battalion has been disbanded, the officers, warrant officers, non-commissioned officers and men have not been lost to the Royal Irish Rifles. The majority have been drafted into other battalions of the Royal Irish Rifles, and will continue to uphold the name and traditions of this regiment with the same spirit, loyalty, and esprit-de-corps as they have done in the 8th-8/9th (Service) Battalions.

G. M. W. MACDONOGH,

Lieut.-General, Adjutant-General to the Forces.

11TH BATTALION ROYAL IRISH RIFLES—108TH BRIGADE.

The battalion was formed in 1914, and on completion of its training was sent to France, landed at Boulogne on October 4, 1915, and was attached to the 12th Brigade, Fourth Division, for instruction, near Mailly Maillet. In November it was transferred to the 12th Brigade, which was posted to the Ulster Division on November 4. With this brigade the battalion underwent training near Pernois.

In December the battalion was transferred back to the 108th Brigade, and in February, 1916, took over part of the line in the Auchonvillers sector. It was here, or opposite Thiepval, till the end of June.

On July 1 the battalion attacked south of the Ancre, and took the first and second lines, but was held up by the German third line, and though it endeavoured to consolidate the second line, this was ultimately lost after heavy fighting, in which the battalion had severe casualties. It was relieved on July 3, and then proceeded to Belgium, taking over part of the Ploegsteert sector on July 23. It spent the rest of 1916 in this area, and was here or a little further north in the opening months of 1917.

On June 7 the battalion was in reserve at first in the attack on Messines Ridge, being employed as "moppers-up" after the capture of the first objective. It had less than 50 casualties.

In July it was moved into the Ypres salient, and took over trenches on August 7 north-east of Ypres. In the attack of August 16, near Fortuin, it was in reserve, but assisted to cover the retirement of the attacking battalions when they were driven back.

Later in August the battalion was moved south, and was in trenches south-west of Cambrai until the offensive of November 20. In this period it had some successes in minor operations, especially on September 21, when it repulsed three hostile raids.

In September the battalion was amalgamated with the 13th Battalion, and redesignated the 11th/13th Battalion Royal Irish Rifles. On the 23rd it took part in the attack near Mouvres, acting in support of the 12th Battalion Royal Irish Rifles, and consolidating the ground gained. It was then moved to Peaucamps in December, and to Douchy in January, 1918. In February, 1918, the battalion was broken up.

In every engagement in which this battalion took part it upheld the brilliant and glorious traditions of the Royal Irish Rifles to which it belonged.

14TH BATTALION ROYAL IRISH RIFLES (Y.C.V.'S)—109TH BRIGADE.

The battalion was formed in September, 1914, and after completing training at Bramshott, was sent overseas in October, 1915, landed at Havre October 6, and proceeded to Amiens. It was first attached for training to the Forty-eighth Division in the Fonquevillers sector, was then (November 4) transferred to the 12th Brigade temporarily, rejoining its original brigade in December.

Most of its early service was spent in the Auchonvillers and Thiepval areas, and on July 1 the battalion made a gallant attack, making considerable progress, and being in the end forced back to our original line, as the division on its flank had failed to get their objective, and so the flank was exposed.

After the fighting of July 1 the battalion was transferred to Flanders, and did duty in the Ploegsteert and neighbouring areas for the rest of 1916.

Up to the end of 1916 the honours awarded to the battalion included one V.C., awarded to Private W. Macfadzean, two M.C.'s, a D.C.M., and five M.M.'s.

During the early part of 1917 the battalion was still in the northern area, being opposite the Messines Ridge when on duty in trenches. In May it made two raids, one on the 22nd being very successful, and in the great attack of June 7 it was conspicuously successful, reaching and securing the German third line—the objective assigned to it. For this it received a D.S.O., two M.C.'s, a D.C.M., and ten M.M.'s.

In the attack of August 16, near Fortuin (northeast of Ypres), the battalion made considerable progress at first, but was compelled to fall back by meeting much uncut wire.

Moving to the southern zone, it did duty in the Hermies sector in September and October, and in the attack on the Hindenburg line (November) it did conspicuously well, gaining its objectives both on November 20-21 with slight loss, and holding on against counter-attacks on the 22nd.

In December the battalion was in trenches in Havrincourt Wood, and then moved further southeast in January, to relieve the French in the St. Quentin sector. On January 30 it received news of the order for its disbandment, which took place in February.

ULSTER DIVISION DISTINCTIONS

The following is the record of decorations won by officers, N.C.O.'s, and men of the Ulster Division for gallantry in the field between October, 1915, and November, 1918:—

VICTORIA CROSS	9
DISTINGUISHED SERVICE ORDER	71
MILITARY CROSS	459
DISTINGUISHED CONDUCT MEDAL	173
MILITARY MEDAL	1294
MERITORIOUS SERVICE MEDAL	118
FOREIGN (FRENCH, BELGIAN, &c.)	312
	2436

To the total has to be added the mentions in despatches, numbering several hundreds, and the award of the C.M.G. and C.B. to a number of the senior officers in various Birthday and New Year Honour lists.

THE KING'S MESSAGE

Acknowledging a loyal message from the Ulster Unionist Council in December, 1918, his Majesty the King sent the following telegram:—

The Right Hon. Sir Edward Carson, Belfast.—I deeply appreciate the congratulations of my loyal Ulster subjects which you have transmitted to me. In these days of rejoicing I recall the deeds of the 36th Ulster Division, which have more than fulfilled the high opinion formed by me on inspecting that force on the eve of its departure for the front. Throughout the long years of struggle, which have now so gloriously ended, the men of Ulster have proved how nobly they fight and die.—Signed,

GEORGE R.I.

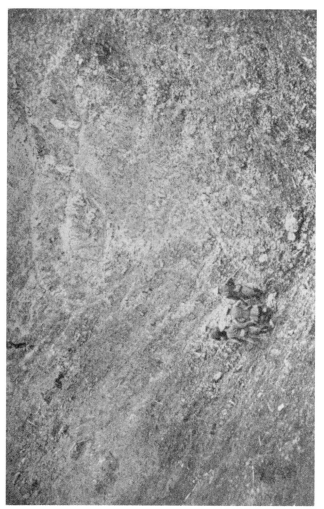

Mine Crater at Messines, round which 8th & 9th Batts. Royal Irish Rifles advanced to the attack on 7th June, 1917.

The Tenth Division at Gallipoli

THE Tenth (Irish) Division, in which Ulster was largely represented, won fame in fields of war far removed from France and Flanders. The East was the scene of its triumphs, and it was not until the closing stages of the war that the remnant of the Division landed at Marseilles and took part in the final crushing of the Hun. The North of Ireland provided five battalions for this great Division, viz:—

5th Battalion Royal Inniskilling Fusiliers,
6th Battalion Royal Inniskilling Fusiliers,
5th Battalion Royal Irish Fusiliers,
6th Battalion Royal Irish Fusiliers (forming the 31st Infantry Brigade), and
6th Battalion Royal Irish Rifles,

which was brigaded in the 29th Brigade with the 5th Royal Irish Regiment, 5th Connaught Rangers, and the 6th Leinster Regiment. The Division was formed early in August, 1914, and in the first rush to the colours many North of Ireland men were posted to its battalions, including a goodly number of the U.V.F., who did not wait for sanction being given to the formation of their own Division in September. The training was carried out in the Dublin district, and subsequently in the vicinity of Basingstoke. General Sir Bryan Mahon was the first Divisional Commander, and it was he who look the Division to Gallipoli, where it received its baptism of fire in August, 1915, being thus the first Irish Division to take the field. The Ulster Brigade landed at dawn on 7th August. Major Bryan Cooper tells the story graphically in the "Irish Soldier." The shore was dark, though here and there flashes of musketry showed where the 11th Division, who had landed first, were pushing back the screen of Turks who had endeavoured to prevent their disembarkation. As the light grew the soldiers could see where they were. From the beach in front of them rose the isolated hummock of Lala Baba; beyond it lay the Salt Lake, dry, shining, and treacherous, bordered by a scrub-covered rolling plain from which stood out the white-washed houses and minarets of the villages of Biyuk Anafarta and Anafarta Saghir. Between the two villages, and nearer to the shore lay the hillock which later acquired the name of Chocolate Hill, and behind them towered the main backbone of the Gallipoli Peninsula, the Ridge of Sari Bair. From the north of the bay inland ran the range of hills known as the Kiretch Tepe Sirt, washed by the sea to the left of it, and commanding the whole Anafarta Plain; while to the south-east was seen the jumble of hills and gullies that has made the name of Anzac immortal.

All this the soldiers saw as they waited for the grunting lighters to come alongside and unload them. The Turkish gunners saw them, too, and shrapnel churned up the sea around them and took its toll on the crowded decks. Disembarkation was hurried; but it was noon, and the sun was blazing with tropical force before Brigadier-General F. F. Hill (formerly of Belfast) was able to collect the Inniskilling and Royal Irish Fusiliers of his own Brigade, and two battalions of the 30th Brigade under the lee of Lala Baba.

At first General Hill's force moved northward across a narrow strip of sand between the sea and the Salt Lake, which was swept by the enemy's fire. Reforming after this unpleasant passage, they turned eastward across a plain covered with prickly scrub, traversed by water-worn gullies, and populated by hostile snipers, whose numbers it seemed impossible to estimate. To the south-east rose the trench-seamed face of their objective, and through the burning afternoon, thirsty and weighed down with their burdens, they pressed towards it. Land mines, shrapnel and high explosives had caused many casualties in the ranks; but when the men came within charging distance of the hill, and the word was passed to fix bayonets, weariness and thirst were forgotten. With an Irish yell, the Inniskillings and Royal Irish Fusiliers, with the Dublins, dashed forward into the enemy's trenches, and before nightfall the whole hill was in their hands.

There followed a week of fruitless fighting, while every day the enemy grew stronger and every day the hope of victory became more faint. At last, however, the Division was concentrated on the beach (where they were still under constant shellfire), and prepared for a new task. There were many gaps in the ranks; the Turks had killed and wounded many, and thirst and privation, dysentery and enteric were making terrible havoc, but the spirit of the men was still high, and they longed for an opportunity of fighting as a Division and showing the world what Irishmen could do. On August 15th the orders came. It was impossible to attack Sari Bair across the Anafarta Plain while the enemy was in possession of the Kiretch Tepe Sirt, so the 10th Division was ordered to attack along both sides of this sharp rocky ridge and drive the Turks off it. On the seaward side all went well. Supported by the guns of two destroyers, the Dublins and Munsters dashed forward magnificently, and hurled the enemy out of his positions. The attack on the southern face was less fortunate; the 5th Inniskilling Fusiliers, who bore the brunt of it, were almost annihilated, and it was found impossible to advance the line. Thus at nightfall on the 15th the position held by the Division resembled an Z; the diagonal running along the crest of the ridge joining the most advanced ground won on the seaward slope, with the original position on the landward side. Tactically, it was not a strong position, as was soon to appear. At 10 p.m. the Turks counter-attacked, but coming to close quarters, were driven off at the point of the bayonet. After this they learnt wisdom, and used weapons against which we were unable to retaliate.

The Turks had grenades, apparently in unlimited numbers, and they rained an unceasing storm of them on our men as they clung to the ridge of the Kiretch Tepe Sirt. Our scanty supply was soon exhausted, and against the bomb, rifle and bayonet were useless, for the bomber lurked out of sight among the rocks, only exposing for a second the hand that sped the missile on its deadly course. Attacked from front and flank alike, the Royal Irish Fusiliers, who held the top bar of the Z, the ground

Chocolate Hill, Gallipoli, Captured by 10th Division in August, 1915.

nearest the sea, were almost wiped out, but the survivors held stubbornly on. On the main ridge the Dublins and Munsters endured nobly the unceasing strain. Here and there men, fevered by inaction, hurled stones at the enemy, while others endeavoured the terrible hazard of catching the Turkish bombs and throwing them back before they exploded. Now and then an officer, hoping to remove some unusually pernicious band of bombers, led a charge across the stony crest, but such attacks were exposed to the enemy's concentrated fire, and melted away in death. There was nothing to be done but to suffer and endure. At nightfall on the 16th the remainder of the two Brigades, mainly the survivors of the men who had charged on the previous day, came up to reinforce their comrades and share their fate. Before sunrise, after another night of horror, it became clear that the position was untenable, and the Irishmen were ordered to withdraw. Suffering agonies from thirst, weakened by dysentery and enteritis, unable to reply to an enemy armed with superior weapons, they had held an untenable position for thirty-six hours, and only left it when they were commanded to do so. The 10th Division had done its duty.

The 6th Battalion Royal Irish Rifles did not take part in this fighting. They had a rough time elsewhere. Separated from the rest of the Division, they disembarked at Anzac on the night of August 5th, and waited in reserve in Shrapnel Gully, while their comrades landed at Suvla. The Rifles were set to hold the ground that had been gained halfway up the precipitous slope of Sari Bair.

Exposed to terrible shell fire, and suffering agonies from thirst, they were in no condition to meet the attack that swept down on them on the morning of the 10th. Again and again the Turks were repulsed, but fresh waves of attackers took their places, and the ranks of the Rifles grew terribly thin. Their colonel, their adjutant, and all their field officers were quickly put out of action; the whole of the Staff of the Brigade, who were with them, were down, and soon a junior officer, who hailed from Belfast, found himself in command of the battalion. The position appeared hopeless, and a retirement was ordered. Even after all they had endured the men were still loath to retire, and when an officer tried to organise a counter-attack they followed him. It was in vain, and the Staff realised that Sari Bair could not be held.

The Division was only a few weeks on the Peninsula, but during that time it lost almost all the officers and most of the men who went out with it from England. The Turks killed many, disease carried off more; but the Division worthily maintained the name of Old Ireland, and none more grandly so than the Ulster Brigade.

SERVIA, SALONIKA, AND MACEDONIA

The remnant of the Tenth Division left Gallipoli in September, 1915. Casualties in the field and disease had decimated the ranks, the 5th Battalion Royal Irish Fusiliers, for instance, mustering only four officers and 160 men before the evacuation. This number was greatly reduced in health by bad and uncongenial food, scarcity of water, and alternate exposure to a burning sun by day and damp cold by night. Suffering was still further increased by the continual strain of action, lack of proper rest and sleep, and by the very heavy digging that was necessary. From first line to beach was under enemy domination, and in the daylight hours every movement brought its bombardment from the heights. That was the theatre of war to which the Division bade adieu, and sailed [to] Lemnos and Mudros to recuperate. Bulgaria had just entered the war, and khaki drill being exchanged for warmer clothing, the Division was ordered to Salonika as part of the Allied Relief Force to aid the Servians. In October the units were all concentrated under Sir Bryan Mahon, and were moved into Servia, the arrangement being that the British were to maintain the position from Salonika to Krivolak and to support the French right, and that if communication with the Servians could not be opened and kept up the Allied Forces were to be withdrawn.

With this object, two battalions of the 10th Division were moved from Salonika on 27th October, and took over the French front from Kosturino to Lake Doiran. The remainder of the Division was sent to Servia on 12th November and following days, and took over the French front eastwards from Kosturino. The task of moving troops into Servia and maintaining them there presented many difficulties. No road exists from Salonika to Doiran, a few miles of road then obtains, which is followed within a few miles by a track only suitable for pack transport. Sir B. Mahon had, therefore, to readjust his transport to a pack scale, and was dependent on a railway of uncertain carrying power to convey back his troops whilst in Servia. Very soon afterwards reinforcements commenced to arrive. During November and the early part of December the 10th Division was holding its position in Servia, and the disembarkation of other divisions was proceeding with difficulty. In order to gain time for the landing of fresh troops at Salonika, and their deployment on the positions selected, Sir Chas. Monro represented to General Sarrail and Sir B. Mahon the urgent need of the divisions withdrawing from Servia being utilised as a covering force, and retaining their ground as such until the forces disembarking were thoroughly in a position to hold their front. It had been evident for some time that the power of resistance of the Servian Armies was broken, and that the Allied Forces could afford them no material assistance. It was also clear from all information received that the position of our troops was becoming daily more precarious owing to a large German-Bulgarian concentration in the Strumniza Valley. General Sarrail proceeded with his withdrawal from the positions he was holding. The Tenth Division operating as it was, as the pivot upon which the withdrawal was effected, was compelled to hold its ground until the French left was brought back. Before the withdrawal was completed the 10th Division was heavily attacked on the 6th, 7th, and 8th December, by superior Bulgarian forces. The troops had suffered considerably from the cold in the Highlands of Macedonia, and in the circumstances conducted themselves very creditably in being able to extricate themselves from a difficult position with no great losses. They had to hold a line of ten miles of mountain with the right flank resting on Lake Doiran, one of the features of which was a spur known as Rocky Peak. It was here that the Ulster Brigade distinguished itself. Before 7 a.m., the enemy, under cover of the mists, had crept up to and rushed an advanced post of the Royal Irish Fusiliers on the peak, their weird cries sounding most uncannily on the damp, heavy air. The possession of this post enabled them to get up machine-guns and bring a deadly fire to bear on part of the line which obviously could not be held much longer. But the Irishmen, by the use of the rifle almost alone, kept off the masses of Bulgars for over nine hours, and then numbers told. In some places the enemy had to be driven back at the point of the bayonet, and in a few localities groups of Bulgars who had effected a lodgment in dead ground up against the trenches could only be effectively dealt with by the use of bombs. The trenches of C Company were entered, and floods of the enemy forced their way along the line in both directions. The few remaining men of C Company, with their surviving officers, fell back and were joined in the ravine by what was left of B Company.

The line soon fell back on the mouth of the Dedli Pass, and after holding this position for three nights and days, the rearguard marched away to make a final stand on the Greco-Serbian Frontier, the 31st (Ulster) Brigade and part of the 29th Brigade, which had been on the right flank, falling back across the line of retreat to cover the old rearguard while it took up its new position. The new rearguard felt little pressure at first, for the blowing up of the bridges in the Pass delayed considerably the enemy advance, but near the northern edge of the Lake of Doiran it had all it could do to stem the invasion of the Bulgars and gain time for those who had gone before to deploy on the new line. The Inniskillings and Irish Fusiliers performed prodigies of valour in the retreat, and reached Salonika in time for Christmas after a fearful march through bleak, open country in torrents of rain, the other brigades having arrived by train from Doiran station. A French General declared that "The rearguard fighting of the Irish in the Servian mountains was one of the most striking feats of arms in the whole war. Against ten times their number they saved the British and French Armies."

For the next five months the Division was recuperating, and at the same time working hard in the genial warmth of a Macedonian spring, in the preparation of the outer defences of Salonika and the organisation of interior lines. It was believed that the Bulgars would attack the town, possession of which would have given them a valuable submarine base. The Division was located about ten kilometres from Salonika, and before the end of May had laid down acres of barbed wire, made miles of trenches, often in the solid rock, and built roads innumerable. Barrosa Day, 1916, sacred to the Royal Irish Fusiliers, was celebrated under the heights of Mount Kotos, where St. Paul preached to the Thessalonians. In June it was evident that the enemy were not going to advance, therefore the Allies pushed forward into Northern Macedonia, the

Ulster Brigade and the 6th Rifles occupying the heights overlooking the Struma valley. In September, 1916, the Division took up elevated positions on the right bank of the Struma, with the enemy on the other side. The Ulster Brigade made a successful reconnaissance in force across the river on 10th September, and various demonstrations and enterprises were carried through in the succeeding weeks. In November the 5th and 6th Battalions of the Royal Irish Fusiliers were amalgamated under Lt.-Col. F. A. Greer, who subsequently commanded the 30th Brigade of the Division. The vacancy in the Brigade was filled by the transfer of the 2nd Battalion of the regiment from the 28th Division. Throughout the summer and autumn the Division suffered severely from malarial fever, which caused more wastage than the enemy. The winter of 1916 and the spring of 1917 were spent in and out of the line, raids being the only excitement the troops enjoyed. The Struma valley was evacuated before the summer, which was spent on the hills overlooking it. In September, 1917, the Division was relieved by the 28th Division, and was ordered to Egypt en route for Palestine, thus bringing to a close two years of Balkan misery.

PALESTINE AND FRANCE

The Division reached Alexandria in the last week of September, and had a week's rest at Ismalia, finally moving along the Suez Canal to Kantara, the base of the Palestine Forces. General Allenby's victorious campagin of 1917-1918 was about to begin, and the task allotted to the Irish troops was the piercing of the enemy's line midway between the towns of Gaza and Beersheba. The Sinai Desert was safely crossed, and though the troops thereafter suffered severely from want of water, they stood the new conditions well. The first serious brush with the enemy was on 6th November, in the attack on Beersheba, the objective of the Ulster Brigade being the Rushdi system, a network of well constructed and strongly wired trenches. The 2nd and 5th Battalions of the Irish Fusiliers led the attack side by side, and displayed such dash that the position was soon in their hands. Next day they took by assault Hareira Tefe Redoubt, one of the strongest in Southern Palestine, shortly after which the Turks were driven clean out of the general Gaza Beersheeba line. The Division then marched westwards across the desert to Belah near the coast, and at the end of November they went northward through the Land of Goschen and the valley of Ajalon. Fighting among the Judaean hills ensued, and in the attack of 9th December, which enveloped Jerusalem, the Division did its share. When the Turks made their great assault east and north of the city, on 27th December, the Irish Division counter attacked with a view to piercing the line and cutting his communications. The Ulster Brigade carried a series of heights forming the ridge that overlooked from the north and west the Wadi, known Biblically as the Valley of Elah, the scene of the historic encounter between David and Goliath. The other brigades did equally well, and the rapidity of the advance turned the Turkish offensive into a hasty withdrawal. January was spent in making the great road which joins the Jerusalem-Nablus road, near Ram-Allah, to the coastal plain, in preparing for the next advance, and in the outpost zone. In the offensive which began on 9th March the Division was on the left flank of the 20th Corps, which was attacked outside the Jerusalem-Nablus Road. The Irish Fusiliers were on the right of the Division and the Inniskillings on the left. The positions to be attacked consisted of a series of strongly held ridges, intersected by great ravines, the ridges extending for miles, and being at points over 3,000 feet high. In this attack the 2nd Battalion Royal Irish Fusiliers captured the formidable stronghold, Sheik Kalrowany, and Hill 2791. The 5th Irish and 5th Inniskilling Fusiliers displayed great heroism in face of heavy fire in capturing and holding on to other hills, the capture of Hill K4 being an especially gallant feat. The final capture of Tiljilia (ancient Gilgal) placed all the objectives allotted for the operations in their hands, and the 31st Brigade had the honour of being the only one that secured all its objectives in the specified time. Another spell of roadmaking and outpost duty followed, and before the next offensive developed the greater part of the division was transferred to France, where the position was serious, Indian troops replacing them. In the middle of May such battalions of the Division as were in being were landed at Marseilles.

In the subsequent operations on the Western front the Division was not strong enough to operate as a whole. This booklet is only concerned with the Ulster units, which were widely scattered. The 5/6th Royal

Irish Fusiliers, for instance, were first sent to the 14th Division in the Merville sector, and at one time were in danger of disbandment. This was averted, and the battalion went to the 30th Division in the south, and then to the 66th Division, and finally to the resurrected 16th Irish Division, which was being organised for the first time since the St. Quentin retreat. The battalion joined this Division in August, 1918, in the La Bassee sector, and took part with it in the subsequent advance. It was bombarded by gas shells at Anchy, and fought afterwards along the La Bassee-Haute Deule Canal and on to the Scheldt, which was crossed on 10th November, and on the following day, when the battalion was at Antoing, the armistice was signed, and the Brigade Commander in a speech expressed his great appreciation of the work done by the unit in France. The Inniskilling battalions were put into the line in the Cambrai sector, and became involved in the severe fighting of October in that region, losing a number of officers and men who had come through the Eastern campaign, including Capt. C. G. Barton, of Port Salon, who had been with the 6th Battalion practically since its formation. The remaining Ulster battalion of the Tenth Division—the 6th Battalion Royal Irish Rifles— never served in France.

Ulster in the 16th Division

FEW divisions of the New Army made a greater name at the front than the 16th Irish Division, commanded by Major-General Hickie. The North of Ireland was represented in that Division, as in the 10th, by an entire brigade, the 49th, composed as follows:—

7th Battalion Royal Inniskilling Fusiliers,
8th Battalion Royal Inniskilling Fusiliers,
7th Battalion Royal Irish Fusiliers,
8th Battalion Royal Irish Fusiliers,

Also one battalion of the Royal Irish Rifles, the 7th, which was a unit in the 48th Brigade. This Brigade also included the famous 6th Battalion Connaught Rangers, in which no fewer than 600 Belfastmen, chiefly from the Falls Road district, served. It was commanded by an Ulsterman, in the person of Lieut.-Col. J. S. Lenox Conyngham, a member of the family of that name which for generations has been settled at Springhill, Moneymore. Another unit of this Brigade, the 6th Battalion Royal Irish Regiment, contained several hundred men from the counties of Londonderry and Tyrone. The Division trained in the south of Ireland, with Fermoy as its headquarters, and prior to its removal to England in 1915 the Ulster Brigade made a short stay at Enniskillen and Finner Camp. Training was completed at Pirbright and Bordon, in the Aldershot command, and in December, 1915, the 47th and 48th

Brigades proceeded overseas. The Ulster Brigade was not up to strength by reason of the fact that prior to the departure of the 10th Division for Gallipoli it had supplied 1,700 trained men to that division. The Brigade was inspected by her Majesty the Queen in January, 1916, and proceeded overseas in that month to join the other brigades. They were put into the line in the Vermelles sector, and soon earned a name for themselves for their excellent discipline and smart raiding. The first severe ordeal which the Division was called upon to undergo took place on the 27th April, 1916, when it was subjected to one of the most intense gas attacks which had ever been launched by the Germans. The appliances for checkmating the use of gas on the British side were not at that time so perfect as they afterwards became, and it was not surprising that there were many casualties. The Inniskilling battalions especially suffered in this attack, and were specially complimented afterwards by the Army Commander, General Chas. Monro, and by the Divisional Commander. During the action on the 27th the Germans rushed the British lines at several places, under cover of their bombardment, and were instantly expelled by the 7th Battalion Royal Inniskilling Fusiliers. An attack was launched on the 29th April, and was again repulsed with great heroism, not a man leaving his post in spite of the awful gassing to which the troops were subjected. This fighting took place at Hulluch, and amongst those who fell were Second-Lieut. F. P. M. Leonard, of Belfast, and Second-Lieut. N. D. Trimble, of Enniskillen.

It is, however, with the attack on Guinchy and Guillemont in the Somme Battle in September, 1916, that the name of the Division is most prominently identified. The 49th Brigade never received its due meed of praise for its work in the terrible first fortnight in September, but none the less it did its duty manfully and well, as its terrible casualty lists show.

Guillemont, which was attacked on the 3rd September, was one of the strongest of all the many fortified villages in the German line, and its capture was the most important achievement of the British since the taking of Pozieries. It was the last uncaptured point in the old German second position between Mouquet Farm and the junction with the French. It was most resolutely defended, since, being close to the point of junction, it compelled a hiatus in the advance of the Allied front. With its fall to the Irishmen, the work of two years was swept away, and in the whole section the enemy were now in new and improvised positions.

On the 9th September the Division again distinguished itself by capturing Guinchy in equally gallant fashion. The attack was delivered at 4-45 in the afternoon, on a broad front, and was one of the few successful attacks of that day. It was followed by a magnificent attack on a moment's notice by the Irish Fusilier battalions on the trenches north of Combles.

Some idea of the severity of the fighting in which the Ulster Brigade and 7th Royal Irish Rifles had come through may be judged from the fact that their casualties ran into four figures. The 8th Inniskillings lost their C.O.,

Troops of 16th Irish Division returning after the capture of Guillemont on 3rd September, 1916.

Lieut.-Col. H. P. Dalzell-Walton, and amongst other officers of the Inniskillings who fell in this fighting were Lieut. T. J. Kennedy, editor the "Northern Standard," Monaghan; Second-Lieut. R. S. Purdy, Second.-Lieut. W. Morgan (Belfast), Second-Lieut. C. A. Crowe (Enniskillen), and many others not directly connected with the province. Lieut.-Col. H. N. Young, D.S.O., of the 7th Inniskillings, was dangerously wounded. The 7th and 8th Royal Irish Fusiliers lost, amongst others killed, Capts. T. G. Fitzpatrick, G. W. Eaton (grandson of a former Belfast R.M.), Lieut. A. E. Kinghan, Lieut. J. P. A. Lane, and Lieut. F. P. H. Harpur; whilst the 7th Battalion Royal Irish Rifles lost, amongst other officers, Major A. B. Cairns, Major A. O. Lash, and Lieut. A. C. Capper. Another officer who fell at the head of his men was Lieut.-Col. Lenox Conyngham, of the Connaught Rangers.

The Division was shortly afterwards taken out of the line to refit, and a few weeks found it with the Second Army in Flanders, where, until the following June, it soldiered with the Ulster Division. The relations between the two were of the happiest character, and there was much friendly rivalry between them when they went over the top simultaneously.

In the great attack on the Messines-Wytschaete Ridge on the morning of 7th June, 1917, the 16th Division was on the left of the Ulstermen, and distinguished itself by the dashing manner in which it captured Wytschaete Wood. Its casualties were not anything like so severe as on the Somme in September. An unnamed wood taken in the course of the fighting by the 7th Royal Inniskilling Fusiliers was afterwards, by the permission of the G.O.C., christened Inniskilling Wood, in token of their valour. It will be recalled that this was the engagement in which the late Major Redmond lost his life, and that he was picked up on the field by men of a field ambulance of the Ulster Division.

Two days after this successful attack the Division was relieved. The event was signalised by the issue of the following message from the Divisional Commander:—

"For over eight months we have held our portion of the line, and we can look back with pride and satisfaction to the record of those months. Neither rain nor snow nor the heat of summer has interfered with the constant work. Long distances, wet roads, cold nights, shortage of fuel, hostile shelling, have all failed to damp the spirit of our men. With gun and howitzer, trench mortar, rifle, machine-gun and bomb, and sometimes with bayonet, we have gradually worn down the boasting enemy; and two days ago, with small losses to the Division, we have completed this chapter of our history by taking from him the Wood and Village of Wytschaete, and the crest of the hill, which means so much for future operations. The Divisional Commander, in congratulating all arms and all ranks of the Division on their victory of June 7th, thanks all the officers, N.C.O.'s and men under his command for their loyalty and help and for their bravery and skill in action. Whatever new work lies before us, it will be tackled with the same endurance, the same cheerfulness, and the same bravery; and again and again the Division and every man in it will justify the right to our motto: Everywhere and always faithful."

In their next great offensive it was ordained that the Irish Division should again fight side by side with the 36th Division, and once more the 49th Brigade and the 7th Royal Irish Rifles worthily upheld the name of Ulster. This was in the bitter fighting which began on 31st July and ended, so far as the Irish troops were concerned, with that awful 16th August, one of the blackest yet most glorious days for Ireland in the whole course of the war. The 49th Brigade were in the thick of the fray on that day. An hour or so before the attack the enemy, as though knowing what was about to come, flung down a tremendous and obstructive barrage, which was answered by our own drum fire—the signal to advance.

The Royal Irish Rifles went forward on the right and the Inniskillings on the left. In front of them were a number of German concrete blockhouses. As the first wave of the assaulting troops advanced Germans rose from ditches and ran back to the shelter of the concrete works, and immediately from those emplacements and from other machine-gun positions behind them swept a fierce enfilade fire, even through the barrage of our shell-fire, which went ahead of the Irish line. Many men in the first wave dropped, but the others kept going, and reached almost as far as they had been asked to go.

The Royal Irish Rifles worked up the Roulers Railway to the level crossing and captured two German officers and thirty prisoners.

On the left the Inniskillings, who had crossed over the Zonnebeke River, made good and rapid progress, capturing two strong redoubts and seizing Hill 37, one of the keys of the position.

So after many hours of frightful fighting the situation was that some scattered groups of the Southern units held out on a far goal with exposed flanks, with some Inniskillings clinging to the slopes of Hill 37, while on the other side of the Zonnebeke River the Ulstermen had been forced off their little hill, and had been unable to get beyond the German chain of concrete houses. The enemy's aeroplanes came over to survey the situation, and flew very low, firing their machine-guns at the advanced posts of Irish lying in shell holes and in the hummocky ground.

Then the enemy launched his counter-attack from the direction of Zonnebeke, and gradually the shattered lines of the Irish fell back, slowly fighting little rearguard actions in isolated groups. Many of them were surrounded and cut off, or had to fight their way back in the night or the dawn of next day.

This day's work and that of the previous few days cost the Division many lives. Some of its finest officers fell, including Lieut.-Col. T. H. Boardman, D.S.O., of the Inniskillings; Capt. H. H. Broadley, Capt. C. N. B. Walker, Lieut. N. H. Woods, and Lieut. T. H. Shaw, of Belfast, all belonging to the Inniskillings; also Lieut. G. Coombes, the famous Army boxer, who was with the Royal Irish Fusiliers; Lieut. J. S. Carrothers, a Co. Fermanagh man, and many others; while the 7th Rifles deplored the loss of Capt. Chas. M'Master, who had begun his military career with the 14th Battalion, the Y.C.V.'s, of the Ulster Division.

The composition of the Division, like that of the 36th Division, had by this time undergone changes, and others were to follow. The 7th and 8th Battalions of the Inniskillings were amalgamated, as were the 7th and 8th Royal Irish Fusiliers, while eventually the 7th Royal Irish Rifles were disbanded. The Division was next actively engaged on the Hindenburg line, where, on 2nd November, 1917, it captured the heights at Croiselles, taking 980 prisoners and putting the 49th German Division out of action. The next big fight of the Diivision was the great retreat of March, in which the 7/8 Inniskillings suffered severely. By this time the number of Ulstermen in the Division had been greatly reduced, and at one time little more than one brigade was composed of Irish regiments. After the retreat the Division was so reduced that it was disbanded. Towards the end of the war the Division was reorganised again with the arrival of certain units of the Tenth Division from the East, and it was in the line on Armistice Day. A great Division it was in its day, and nobly did it uphold the fame of Irishmen as fighters.

Frezenberg, the scene of the attack of the Sixteenth and Ulster Divisions on 16th August, 1917.

The Old Contemptibles

THE story of the regular battalions of the Ulster regiments, with the exception of the 2nd Battalion Royal Irish Fusiliers, is, after 1917, the story of the Ulster Division, in which were finally incorporated the 1st and 2nd Battalions Royal Inniskilling Fusiliers, the 1st and 2nd Battalions Royal Irish Rifles, and the 1st Battalion Royal Irish Fusiliers. The doings of these famous battalions with the 36th Division in 1918 have already been referred to, but a few facts as to their work in the mixed divisions, in which they spent the greater part of the war, should be placed on record. At the outbreak of the war, in accordance with custom, one of the line battalions of each regiment was abroad and the other at home. The three battalions which formed part of the original B.E.F. were the 2nd Royal Inniskilling Fusiliers, 2nd Battalion Royal Irish Rifles, and 1st Battalion Royal Irish Fusiliers, but the 1st Inniskillings (from India), 1st Rifles (from Aden), and 2nd Royal Irish Fusiliers (from India) were so speedily in the fray that they, too, are part of the Old Contemptibles, that noble army which gathered the spears of the Prussian legions into its bosom, and, in perishing, saved Europe.

THE ROYAL INNISKILLING FUSILIERS

The 1st Battalion of the Royal Inniskilling Fusiliers, the grand old 27th Foot, left Bombay on 9th December, 1914, in command of Lieut.-Col. F. G. Jones, landed at Avonmouth on 10th January, 1915, and was billeted at

Rugby from 11th January until its departure overseas as a unit of the 87th Brigade of the 29th Division, which was destined to become famous. The Division reached Gallipoli in April, landing on X Beach, and establishing themselves in an entrenched position, they had their share of the desperate work that followed in the next three weeks. Sir Ian Hamilton's first despatch showed that between the landing and the 5th May the British losses in the peninsula were—2,167 killed, 8,219 wounded, and 3,593 missing. The Inniskillings furnished their quota to the toll, including their C.O. During practically the entire of its stay on the peninsula the battalion was never out of fire. But it displayed qualities of the highest order, especially in the attack of 28th June southeast of Krithia, when Capt. G. R. O'Sullivan and Sergeant Jas. Somers, both since dead, won the Victoria Cross. In the early days of July, and again in the severe fighting of August, when they lost heavily at Scimitar Hill, the old 27th did well against fearful odds, but no one was sorry to leave the peninsula before the winter set in, when the evacuation took place.

The battalion reached Egypt after the evacuation of the peninsula in January, 1916, and after a period of rest the 29th Division was ordered to France, where it saw very hard fighting, in which the 1st Inniskillings, who disembarked at Marseilles on 18th March, 1916, were always to the fore. The Division was to the immediate left of the Ulsters in the great 1st of July attack, and it was a curious coincidence that the 2nd Inniskillings were, in the 32nd Division, on the immediate right of the Ulsters on that day. The Inniskillings were in the van of the attack on the right of their Division, and they were speedily in the German first line opposite Beaucourt and Beaumont Hamel. The Germans had fortified that part of the line for many months, and had assembled north-east and south-east of it a formidable collection of artillery and machine-guns. The advance of the troops was delayed by the fact that the wire had not been completely cut, and by the fact that the dug-outs were found to be full of lurking Germans, who had intended to rush out and attack the stormers in the rear, but who were discovered in time, and had to fight for their lives. The deadly flanking machine-gun fire caused numerous casualties, and it was recognised during the forenoon that only a defensive line could be held. The losses all round were so severe that a renewal of the assault was out of the question, but the holding of the enemy on this part enabled the British and French in the south to achieve brilliant success. As Lieut.-General Sir Aylmer Hunter-Weston, the Corps Commander, said in his message afterwards—"Though we did not do all that we hoped to do, you have more than pulled your weight. It was a magnificent display of courage, worthy of the best traditions of the British race." Amongst the fallen was Lieut.-Col. R. C. Pierce, the Inniskillings' Commanding Officer, a gallant Ulsterman of long service in the old regiment.

Thereafter the 1st Battalion saw alternate spells of fighting and training, taking part in various engagements. One of the smartest of these was at Le Transloy on the morning of 29th January, 1917, when the battalion moved into a broken sector of trenches below Bapaume. The village was on the main Bapaume-Peronne road. The C.O. was now Lieut.-Col. R. R. Willis, of the Lancashire Fusiliers, who had won the V.C. at the Gallipoli landing. The battalion attacked at dawn, with an English unit, on a front of two-thirds of a mile, and swept on to the second German line, capturing 200 prisoners, and wresting another strip from the enemy. It was a brilliant attack, and won for the Inniskillings great praise. To follow the battalion throughout the remainder of the year would require a volume. On every part of the line it did its duty nobly and well.

The 29th Division was one of the divisions that bore the brunt of the prolonged struggle known as the Battle of Arras, which was opened on 9th April, 1917, when the British attacked on a wide front, including the Vimy Ridge, that grim hill which dominates the plain of Douai and the coalfields of Lens—and the German positions round Arras. It was in the second phase of the battle, which began on 23rd April that the Inniskillings had their hardest ordeal. They were south of the Scarpe, and in the attack on the Oppy line, which protected the Hindenburg line, they met with a desperate resistance. Attack and counter-attack were the order of the day, and men who survived that awful fighting around Monchy, Guemappe, and Fontaine les Croiselles will never forget the terrible machine gun and artillery fire to which they were subjected. All the dogged qualities of the British infantry were tried in this struggle, and they prevailed in the end, the Hindenburg line being smashed.

In the Cambrai battle of November, 1917, the battalion again distinguished itself, and the then C.O., Lieut.-Colonel J. Sherwood Kelly, of the Norfolks, won the V.C. by his signal bravery at Marcoing, largely through which the battalion captured its objective. The desperate defence of Masnieres by the 29th Division in this battle is one of the epics of the war, and was the subject of a special order to the G.O.C., General De Lisle, from Sir Douglas Haig, thanking him for the magnificent services rendered during two days and a night, by the Division, which included the Inniskillings. Shortly after this battle the battalion was transferred to the 36th Division, and on 19th January it met the 2nd Battalion for the first time in the war. The work of the battalion with the 36th Division has already been dealt with.

2nd BATTALION ROYAL INNISKILLING FUSILIERS

The 2nd Battalion Royal Inniskilling Fusiliers went overseas in August, 1914, as part of the Eleventh Brigade of the Fourth Division. Stationed at Dover when hostilities broke out, it disembarked at Havre on 24th August, and on the following morning, on arrival at Bertry, heard the guns of the British First and Second Army Corps in action against Von Kluck. The British were retreating from Mons, and the Fourth Division was given the task of protecting the left flank. On the morning of 26th August one-half of the battalion, which was under Major C. A. Wilding, was attacked and suffered severely in the region of Le Cateau. The entire battalion participated in the retreat towards Paris, and in the hardships of that time and the glory of the subsequent advance on the Marne, and the vigorous trench warfare on the Aisne, the Inniskillings had their share. The battalion crossed the Marne on 7th September and the Aisne on 13th September. Major Wilding succeeded to the command, Lieut.-Col. H. P. Hancox having received a staff appointment.

On 6th October the battalion was relieved by the French at St. Marguerite, and on 15th October it arrived at Hazebrouck, being in action at Meteran next day. On 14th it entered Bailleul, then Ploegsteert, Le Gheer, Houplines, Armentieres, and on 31st October it relieved the Indian troops at Messines. Capts. Roe and Auchinleck were killed at Le Gheer on 21st October. Moving and fighting characterised the entire of this trying winter, in the course of which the battalion had the honour of giving the first N.C.O. to the officers' ranks for service in the field during the war. This was Sergt. H. H. Kendrick, who was promoted second-lieutenant, and in less than two years was lieut. colonel in temporary command of a battalion of the Suffolk Regiment.

After the winter in the trenches the Inniskillings were called upon to undergo a severe ordeal in the great offensive of 15th May, 1915, at Richebourg, or Festubert, as it is sometimes called. It was then in the Fifth Brigade.

The strength of the battalion going into action on that night was well over 1,000, not including many men left with the transport. Captain J. N. Crawford was in command, and it was Capt. C. C. Hewitt, with "D"

Company, that first succeeded in storming and taking the German trenches. The battalion did very well, and "D" Company's exploit was magnificent. The attack along the whole division line was timed for 11-30 p.m., and shortly after that hour the crack of the German rifles and hammering of the machine guns began, and rose till it reached a roar. At the same time the ground was lit up by white, green, and red flare lights, the latter being the German call for artillery action, which was not long in coming, for soon the whole of the breastworks seemed to be deluged in a rain of bursting shells. Our attack was divided into two parts, by a cinder road and a deep ditch running at right angles to our breastworks. Although our artillery had bombarded the German breastworks for days, and had laid them flat, yet they had neither dissipated the Germans nor their courage, as their lines were full of men when we arrived up to them. "D" Company, however, overcame all obstacles, and managed to hold on until the arrival of reinforcements, when the captured lines were consolidated. Some hours after the remains of the battalion were withdrawn on being relieved. The total losses were twenty officers and about 700 men.

The following orders were read to the troops on parade on 30th May by order of Lieutenant-Colonel C. A. Wilding, Commanding 2nd Royal Inniskilling Fusiliers:—

Officer Commanding,
2nd Royal Inniskilling Fusiliers.

General Sir Douglas Haig, K.C.B., K.C.I.E., K.C.V.O., A.D.C., General Commanding 1st Army, has personally desired me to thank all ranks of the 5th Infantry Brigade for their great gallantry and hard work during the recent operations, which, although they did not result in any great gain of country, had other far-reaching effects and achieved important results.

And thanks of General Joffre have also been sent to the 1st Army for the way in which they have drawn the enemy's troops away from other parts, thus enabling the French to carry out plans which could not otherwise have been successful.

(Sd.), A. A. CHICHESTER,
Brigadier-General, Commanding 5th Infantry Brigade.

23/5/15.

(2)

Major-General Sir Charles Monro, G.O.C. 1st Army Corps, who visited the Commanding Officer on Monday last, wished to congratulate all ranks of the battalion on their fine performance on the night of the 15th-16th May. He has known the battalion for a long time, and has every confidence that they will do in the future as they have done in the past.

(Sd.), C. A. M. ALEXANDER, Captain,
A/Adjt. 2nd Royal Inniskilling Fusiliers.

27/5/15.

After a period of service as army troops, the battalion joined the 13th Brigade of the 5th Division on 18th November, 1915, and on 4th February, 1916, Major J. N. Crawford assumed command, vice Lieut.-Col. C. A. Wilding, who had got a brigade. The next move was to the 96th Brigade, 32nd Division, which was on the right of the Ulster Division on 1st July. In that terrible struggle the Inniskillings had considerable losses. They were a supporting battalion, and were in a veritable furnace trying to keep in touch with the storming battalions, which were swallowed up in the German lines. The odds were impossible, but it was not their fault that the attack did not produce all the results looked for. On the night of 10th July, the battalion again distinguishing itself. Orders were received that part of an enemy trench that formed a re-entrant in the line had to be taken. This the Inniskillings did after desperate hand-to-hand fighting, and subsequently repulsed two furious attacks by the enemy. The 26th August, 1916, the second anniversary of the landing, found the battalion in the trenches, but with few of the old brigade. Lieutenant and Quartermaster Lumsden was the only officer serving at that time who came abroad as an officer of the battalion in 1914. In May, 1917, Lieut.-Col. Crawford was invalided home, but rejoined later in the year. Throughout 1917 the battalion was constantly in action, but it was destined for further hot work in 1918, when it became a unit of the Ulster Division, as already recorded.

1st Battalion Royal Irish Rifles

THE 1st Battalion Royal Irish Rifles landed at Liverpool on 22nd October, 1914, after 17½ years' service in the East, and on 5th November left Southampton for France. On 15th November the battalion went into the trenches for the first time, losing three men killed, and on the following day had 28 casualties. The usual tours of duty in the trenches lasted until the end of February, the casualties being two officers killed and 106 other ranks killed and wounded, while there were several hundred cases of frost-bite. The first big engagement of the old 83rd was the Battle of Neuve Chapelle on 10th March, 1915. The Rifles were to go through the Lincolns, who were to take the first line of trenches, and take the second line. No sooner had the Lincolns reached the first line than the Ulstermen dashed forward as one man, and with a yell that could be heard for miles, were through the Lincolns and the German first line, and in a few minutes were over the barbed wire and the brook, and had taken the German second and third lines, and were right through, killing or capturing every German in these lines, and then on to the village, which with the assistance of the Rifle Brigade was also taken. It was here the battalion gloriously avenged the brave heroes of the 2nd Battalion, who had died in these trenches in October last at the hands of overwhelming hordes of Huns, after keeping them at bay for twelve days. There was now nothing more for the battalion to do but dig in and consolidate the ground won. In this attack on the 10th, the casualties sustained were not heavy in comparison with the work done, some 6 officers and 50 or 60 other ranks being killed and wounded.

On the 11th, however, the enemy counter-attacked, and the Rifles suffered rather heavily, and on the 12th their attack was again pushed forward. This time they met a thoroughly organised opposition, and every inch of ground gained cost heavily in life and wounds. It was here Colonel Laurie fell, gallantly leading the battalion, with his adjutant, Captain O'Halloran Wright, Captain Hutcheson, Captain Colles, and many more.

The battalion continued in the fighting line at Neuve Chapelle for 12 days, during which time it lost 9 officers killed, 9 wounded, and 400 non-commissioned officers and men. The part taken by the battalion in this fight was never officially recognised, probably owing to the loss of the C.O., but the deeds performed by all ranks were well fitted to rank side by side with the many splendid acts performed by the battalion in the days of the Peninsular and Mutiny.

After Neuve Chapelle the battalion had a fairly quiet time. About the 10th April, however, we again went into the trenches, the first night in being marked by the death of Capt. W. M. Lanyon, of Belfast, who had just arrived from home with the reinforcements.

On the 9th May—just two months to the day after Neuve Chapelle—the Rifles marched out to take up their position in the assembly trenches for another offensive, this time at Fromelles. On this occasion the battalion was allotted the leading line, with the Rifle Brigade on the right, and, after the bombardment, at the given signal the battalion dashed forward, but, alas, it was found that the bombardment had been very ineffectual, and the enemy were quite prepared. The moment the Rifles reached the top of their own parapet a perfect hail of German machine gun and rifle fire swept the parapet from end to end, and many a gallant fellow, including several officers, went down in that first rush. However, the battalion pushed on, and in spite of being raked from flank to flank and in front by rifle and machine gun fire, they gained their objectives, but at a heavy loss. This fight bereaved many Belfast families, the officers who fell including Lieut. J. S. Martin, Second-Lieuts. A. M'Laughlin and A. W. Bourke, all of Belfast. The commanding officer, Lieut.-Col. O. C. Baker, also lost his life.

After the Battle of Fromelles the battalion returned to billets to refit, and at the beginning of June the battalion took over trenches in front of Laventie, and Lieut.-Colonel R. A. C. Daunt, D.S.O., assumed command. On September 25 the battalion was in support in the attack (in conjunction with Battle of Loos) on Le Brideaux, casualties being 100 officers and men. In November the Rifles went out to rest over Christmas at Sercus. January again saw them in the line near Fromelles. On 27th March, 1916, they entrained for the south, and a fortnight later took over the line opposite La Boiselle. On 11th April, after a very heavy bombardment, the enemy raided the battalion. The attack was beaten off, but our losses were nearly 90 other ranks, killed, wounded and missing. The German official account of the raid, captured some time afterwards, commenced as follows:—"The regiment of Royal Irish Rifles created a most favourable impression both by their physique and their mode of repelling an assault." On June 12th, 1916, Lieut.-Colonel C. C. Macnamara took over command of the battalion, and was commanding on July 1st when the battalion attacked Ovillers and sustained exceedingly heavy casualties, amounting to 18 officers, including both the Commanding Officer and Adjutant, and 440 other ranks. On July 3rd the battalion moved by train to Bethune area, and a week later took over the Hohenzollern Redoubt, the battalion then being under command of Lieut.-Colonel E. C. Lloyd, D.S.O., R.I. Regt. October 11th found the battalion moving to the Somme, and on October 23rd it was engaged in a fierce action on the Le Boeufs-Morval line, with weather conditions at the worst. The battalion at the period did not number more than 250 men. November and December was spent at Laleu, west of Amiens, in billets. In January the battalion returned to the Somme area, and on March 17th moved forward in pursuit of the enemy, who were retiring to the Hindenburg line. In June the battalion moved to Ypres salient, and on July 31st took part in the 3rd Battle of Ypres, and sustained heavy casualties, amounting to 16 officers and 350 other ranks, including the Colonel, Lieut.-Colonel A. D. Reid (Royal Inniskilling Fusiliers), who had been commanding the battalion since June. On August 16th the battalion was again in action, under command

Battered German Trenches taken at Ovillers (Somme Battle), where 1st Royal Irish Rifles lost heavily on 1st July, 1916.

of Lieut.-Col. M'Carthy O'Leary, D.S.O., M.C. (R.I. Fusiliers), the casualties again being heavy, all officers except one (the Adjutant, Captain G. H. P. Whitfield) being either killed or wounded, and 230 other ranks. In September the battalion, under command of Lieut.-Col. J. H. Kirkwood, D.S.O. (Household Cavalry) held the Ploegsteert trenches, and in October were moved on to the Passchendaele Ridge, and took part in the battle on December 1st, 1917. For the work in the Battle of Ypres the battalion was highly praised by Divisional and Corps Commanders and by the Commander-in-Chief himself. The battalion spent its last year with the Ulster Division, and reference to its doings will be found in connection with that Division.

2ND BATTALION ROYAL IRISH RIFLES

Lieut.-Colonel (now Major-General) W. D. Bird, C.B., C.M.G., D.S.O., A.D.C., took the 2nd Battalion Royal Irish Rifles to the front from Tidworth in August, 1914, as part of the Seventh Brigade of the Third Division. They were in action right away at Mons, and in the subsequent battles of the Marne and the Aisne they were conspicuously engaged. The first officer to fall was Second-Lieut. H. C. Magenis, of Finvoy, and among others was Major C. R. Spedding, son of the late Dr. Spedding, of Belfast. Colonel Bird lost a leg at the Aisne. On 28th October and succeeding days the battalion was severely tested at Neuve Chapelle, when it was bombarded repeatedly in the trenches, but held its ground splendidly. General Smith-Dorrien, the Corps

Commander, complimented the officers and men for their bravery, recording that—

> During an attack on the 7th Infantry Brigade the enemy came to close quarters with the Royal Irish Rifles, who repulsed them with great gallantry with the bayonet. The commander wishes to compliment the regiment on its splendid feat, and directs that all battalions shall be informed of the circumstance of his high appreciation of the gallantry displayed.

Capt. T. J. Reynolds, who had just come out from the adjutancy of the 3rd Battalion; Capt. H. A. Kennedy, Capt. H. O. Davis, of Holywood; Lieut. V. T. T. Rea, of Belfast, and other officers, fell in the fighting of this period. Major J. W. Alston was killed in the following spring, when Lieut.-Col. G. A. Weir, 3rd Dragoon Guards, was appointed to the command, and led the battalion in the great offensive of Loos on 25th September, 1915, which partially failed owing to the shell shortage. On that occasion the Rifles, notwithstanding the enemy's preparations, not only pierced the German lines, but actually held their first line trenches for twenty-four hours, but on account of the corps on their flanks failing to achieve their object they were unfortunately obliged to retire to their own lines, having no one to support their flanks.

The Divisional Commander, addressing the battalion afterwards on its transfer to another area, said in the course of his speech:—"You have a splendid fighting record throughout the campaign, being complimented by Sir John French and General Smith-Dorrien in corps orders. The fighting in this part of the line during the last few months has been very severe, and this battalion has made history. When the history of the campaign has been written the name of the 2nd Battalion Royal Irish Rifles will be written in large print. Your commanding officer, Colonel Weir, has been promoted to a brigade, due largely to the conduct of the battalion on the 25th September, 1915. Your Brigadier was ordered to hold the Germans in the Ypres salient while the other corps made the attack further south. You attacked the strongest position in the enemy's line. We had not enough artillery ammunition in our line to give you more support. The result was that the Germans' hidden machine-guns and cleverly-laid barbed wire traps were not demolished entirely. All the big gun ammunition was required farther south. Your clever demonstration in front of this part of the line brought all the enemy's reserves to this point, thereby facilitating the offensive towards Loos. In fact the enemy were prepared to attack, but was half an hour too late."

Amongst the officers of the battalion killed in this fighting were Capt. W. P. O'Lone, of Belfast; Second-Lieuts. K. and M. Ross, of Belfast; Second-Lieut. J. G. Caruth, of Ballymena, and Second-Lieut. W. L. Orr, of Larne. Capt. R. J. O'Lone. one of the three officers who came out of the ordeal unwounded, was killed on 11th November following, and in January, 1916, Lieut. E. Workman, son of Mr. Frank Workman, of Belfast, was mortally wounded. The battalion served in various parts of the line, notably on the Somme, where Capt. W. A. Smiles and Lieut. W. C. M'Connell, of Belfast, lost their lives. In the Messines-Ypres fighting from June, 1917, and following months, the Rifles had some of their hardest fighting. In the attack of 7th June the battalion captured its objective, and extricated another unit from difficulties, through the skilful leadership of Lieut.-Col. H. R. Goodman.

The losses of the battalion were exceptionally severe in August, when the Germans poured tons of high explosives into the British lines. Lieut. S. V. Morgan, the old Adjutant of the 3rd Battalion, was killed in the course of this fighting. Leaving the 25th Division in September, the Rifles went to the Third Army, and were posted to the 108th Brigade of the Ulster Division, whose headquarters had been transferred to Ytres. With this Division they served till the end of the war. In all, the battalion had over 100 officers and 2,000 other ranks killed in action, while the honours awarded numbered close on 400.

1st Battalion Royal Irish Fusiliers

THE 1st Battalion Royal Irish Fusiliers, with a strength of 27 officers and 1,008 other ranks under the command of Lieut.-Col. D. W. Churcher, disembarked at Boulogne on 23rd April, 1914, and after a short rest in camp, proceeded to the theatre of operations. Prior to going to France the battalion had been stationed at Shorncliffe.

On the evening of the 25th August, 1914, the Fusiliers engaged with the enemy for the first time. On the morning of the 26th August, the battalion took part in the Le Cateau-Cambrai action, subsequently retiring before superior forces of the enemy. Heavy fighting ensued, the losses being 8 officers and approximately 200 other ranks.

On 4th September, the enemy having been brought to a standstill, and afterwards forced to retire, the battalion, in co-operation with other forces, followed up in pursuit, inflicting heavy losses on the enemy, in the action of the Aisne which followed, the battalion suffered pretty severely, with approximate casualties of 8 officers and about 150 men.

After the action of the Aisne, the battalion proceeded North, and took part in the battle of Armentieres, which was wrested from the enemy by the "Faughs." The enemy having prepared strong defences in this region, trench warfare was adopted, and in the weeks that followed very little activity was displayed on either side. It was during the stay of the battalion in this sector that Private

Robert Morrow, of Newmills (near Dungannon), Co. Tyrone, earned the Victoria Cross. This young soldier in spite of the enemy's consistent shell fire and within their full view, rescued from imminent danger of death six comrades who were badly wounded from shellfire, carrying each one, in turn, back to a place of safety. During the period of trench warfare several drafts of reinforcements arrived, these brought the unit once more to fighting strength and enabled it to play so fine a part in the second battle of Ypres. This was fought during the month of April, 1915, and assumed its worst character on the 25th of that month, when, under cover of poison gas, the enemy sought by this method to "drive in" the defending forces. The 10th Brigade, of which the battalion formed part, bore the brunt of this struggle, and after a heroic stand brought the enemy to a halt. The losses in this engagement were severe, amounting approximately to 10 officers and 500 other ranks. For this engagement, the battalion was personally thanked by Field-Marshal Sir John French, then commanding the Expeditionary Force. From now onwards the battalion remained in the Ypres sector, and subsequently took part in the second gas attack, May 2nd, again suffering very severely, but still held on to the sector alloted as their defence line. After the latter action the efforts of the enemy somewhat diminished, and the battalion was finally relieved and sent South to the Somme district. Lieut.-Col. A. R. Burrowes, who had assumed command from Lieut.-Col. D. W. Churcher earlier in the campaign, now left to take up a staff appointment.

The battalion arrived and took over a sector of the line from the French in the Somme. Matters were quiet here, and enabled the battalion, through the arrival of reinforcements, to prepare itself for active operations once more.

Major G. Bull was now in command of the battalion. Later Major R. J. Kentish, D.S.O., took over command, Major Bull having been ordered to assume command of the 12th Royal Irish Rifles—a battalion of the 36th (Ulster Division), which previous to this, had been attached to the Fusiliers in the line for instructional purposes. After a short period in command, Major (T/Lieut.-Col.) R. J. Kentish proceeded to take up a staff appointment, and Captain R. B. Neill assumed temporary command. On 20th November, 1915, Mr. John Redmond visited the Battalion.

The winter of 1915 passed quietly. The spring of 1916 found the battalion still located in the Somme, and towards the middle of March a new sector of the line was taken over in this region. Major W. A. V. Findlater had now assumed command. Life in the new sector was very quiet until about the middle of March, when plans for a daylight raid on the enemy's defences were contemplated. For about a week prior to the date set apart for the raid, nightly trips were made into "No Mans' Land," and carried as far forward as within a few yards of the enemy's front line system. Thanks to great co-operation of all ranks of the battalion in maintaining the greatest secrecy concerning the proposed stunt at four o'clock on the afternoon of the 16th April, the

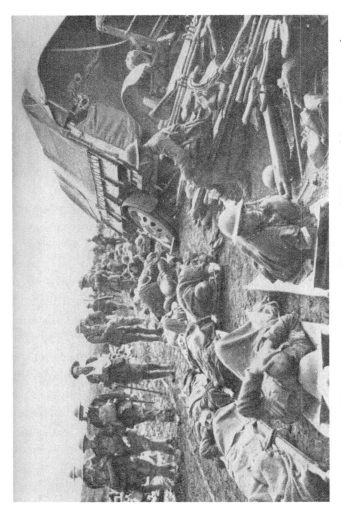

Typical Battlefield Scene — Wounded on Menin Road (Ypres Battle) awaiting removal.

raiding party, which consisted of about 1 officer and 27 other ranks, led by Lieut. N. Russell, of Lisburn, entered the enemy's front line system, bombing the dugouts, shooting and bayoneting in addition no fewer than 63 of the enemy, the raiders' casualties being only one man slightly wounded. For this raid the battalion was specially thanked by the Army Corps Commander, and subsequently mentioned in official dispatches by the Commander-in-chief. Lieut.-Col. R. G. Shuter, D.S.O., who had commanded the battalion previous to the raid and had proceeded to assume temporary command of the 10th Infantry Brigade, now returned and took over command of the battalion from Major R. B. Neill. Lieut.-Col. R. G. Shuter, D.S.O., was subsequently promoted Brigadier-General, and assumed command of the 109th Infantry Brigade. Major W. A. V. Findlater once more assumed command of the battalion, which remained in this sector of the line, and during the intervals of relief from the front line, continued to train energetically. Through the incessant artillery bombardments of the enemy both on the trench defence system and on the occupied billets, the battalion suffered many casualties.

No further actions of any importance occurred, and in the middle of June the battalion was withdrawn from the line to Corps Reserve, to enable training to be carried out, and to rehearse their part in the coming offensive of July the 1st, 1916.

The battalion under the command of Lieutenant-Colonel W. A. V. Findlater, moved to the reserve point on 26th June, and there awaited the order for final march to the assembly positions.

On 1st July, 1916, the battalion had taken up its position in assembly trenches opposite Beaumont-Hamel-Serre, and after the defences in front were demolished by a mine, the 10th Brigade began to move. The enemy, who evidently had been well aware of our intentions, had concentrated a formidable force of men and artillery, and a desperate battle ensued.

The Fusiliers, who were in support to the Seaforth Highlanders, were heavily shelled on their way from their assembly to the front line system. By mid-day the battle had developed furiously, and many hand to hand encounters with the enemy had taken place. Towards evening a company of the battalion, assisted by a company of the Seaforth Highlanders, had, through superb courage and determination, forced their way into the enemy's third line system, the remaining three companies advancing according to plan. By nightfall the position on the flanks did not permit of the battalion holding its position, consequently had to take up its original position. The enemy made several attempts to dislodge it from its system by means of strong counter-attacks, each of which was successfully repulsed. Although everything that had been expected of this battle did not materialise, the power and the will to conquer still remained. Never did troops advance to battle in greater spirits than those which sallied forth on the 1st July, 1916. The following is an extract from a circular letter issued by the Corps Commander, Lieut.-General Sir A. Hunter-Weston (who afterwards visited the battalion and personally thanked them for the part they had played so well:—

"Officers, non-commissioned officers and men of the 1st Battalion Royal Irish Fusiliers, it is impossible for me to express fully my admiration for the splendid courage, determination and discipline displayed by you all. We had the most difficult part of the line to attack. The Germans had fortified it with the greatest skill for many months, and had their best troops manning the points of your attack. They had collected on your front a formidable concentration of artillery and machine guns. Although we did not do all we expected, we have more than pulled our weight, and with such men as you, we are sure to pull off a glorious victory in the end. I salute each officer, non-commissioned officers, and men of the battalion as comrades-in-arms, and am proud to have such a band of heroes in the corps under my command."

The battalion returned to the Ypres salient after operations on the Somme. This was the most deadly point of the British front. Thus, both in and out of the line very little rest was enjoyed, the enemy constantly making local gas attacks. The battalion again moved South and occupied a portion of the line in the Le Transloy sector. On the 12th October an assault was made on the enemy positions in this region. The result proved very adverse, as the enemy had his defences well supplied with machine guns and assisted by a barrage of powerful intensity, he succeeded in maintaining his positions. The losses in this engagement (which only lasted 3 hours) were tremendous—14 officers and 300 other ranks. Having only 8 officers and about 250 men left, the battalion was withdrawn, and proceeded to a camp in the rear.

The winter of 1916 passed quietly. Brevet Lieut.-Col. A. B. Incledon-Webber, D.S.O., was now in command. On the 1st April, 1917, the battalion prepared to take part in the Battle of Arras. Strength at this juncture was 20 officers and 700 other ranks. The battalion assaulted, in conjunction with the Seaforth Highlanders, positions east of Fampoux. The attack was carried out in face of considerable opposition. The battalion suffered severely from enfilade machine gun fire, eventually reaching their objectives and consolidating.

The casualties in this action were 7 officers and 360 other ranks, the depth of the advance being a little over 7 miles. A further attack was made in this region, after the battalion had received reinforcements. A strongly fortified position known as Roeux Chemical Works was the objective. The fight on this occasion was of a furious nature, the battalion just managing to attain their objective by overcoming the enemy's resistance in a series of bayonet fights. Very severe casualties were inflicted on the enemy, their evacuated trenches being filled with their dead. The battalion suffered heavily, losing no fewer than 9 officers and 230 other ranks.

After this battle the battalion was withdrawn to Corps Reserve for re-organisation purposes and training.

On 2nd August, 1917, the Fusiliers bade "Good Bye"

to the 4th Division, in which it had served since the commencement of the campaign. Their departure was deeply felt, especially by their old friends, the Seaforth Highlanders, with whom they had fought side by side in every battle in which the division had taken part, and with whom the spirit of comradeship had become deeply rooted. The 36th (Ulster) Division was the new destination of the "Faughs."

Nothing of any importance occurred from now until the Battle of Cambrai on 25th November, 1917. In this action the battalion took a prominent part. In support to the 10th Royal Irish Rifles it moved forward and attacked the enemy's positions, gaining its objectives, but again suffering heavy casualties. The losses on this occasion were 8 officers and 225 other ranks. It was in this engagement that the Chaplain—the Reverend Father Donohoe did such splendid work, going round the front line encouraging all, and assisting in carrying down wounded. For this action he was awarded the Military Cross.

Brevet Lieut.-Col. A. B. Incledon-Webber had now left the battalion on promotion to Brigadier-General, and Lieut.-Col. S. U. L. Clements was in command from before the battle of Cambrai, he in turn relinquishing on arrival of Lieut.-Col. M. J. Furnell.

The winter of 1917 was very severe, and during the stay of the battalion in the line many casualties were sustained. Reference to the subsequent work will be found in the account of the Ulster Division.

On 28th March, 1919, the Cadre under the command

of Lieut-Col. H. W. D. MacCarthy O'Leary, D.S.O., M.C., embarked at Dunkerque and disembarked at Southampton. Total strength of the party, 6 officers and 52 other ranks. The following represents approximately the number of decorations earned by the battalion during the campaign:—Victoria Crosses, 1; Distinguished Service Order, 13; Military Crosses, 33; Distinguished Conduct Medals, 38; Military Medals, 88; M.S.M.'s, 5; Bars to D.S.O.'s, 1; Bars to Military Crosses, 8; Bars to D.C.M.'s, 4; Bars to Military Medals, 11; Bars to M.S.M.'s, nil.

The total casualties of the battalion during the war were 94 officers killed and 306 wounded, other ranks killed, 2,013; wounded, 5,080.

2nd BATTALION ROYAL IRISH FUSILIERS

The 2nd Battalion Royal Irish Fusiliers has never received the full record of publicity which its services deserve. In the earlier stages of the campaign it was but a unit in an English division, and later on it was part of the Salonika Army, where it fought both disease and Turks for a lengthened period. When war broke out the battalion was in India. Transferred to England, it was rapidly equipped for the front as part of the 28th Division, and by January, 1915, was in the trenches round St. Eloi. The men fresh from the tropics had a very severe time. Many were ill with fever, and the cold, wet weather sent scores of men into hospital, while frost-bite was also rife. The trenches in this sector had been taken over from the French, and according to British ideas were rather sketchy. The Germans, then in their might, were very active, and the Fusiliers with the other units of the Division had a very bad time with bombardments and attacks. They stuck to their guns gamely, and inflicted numerous losses on the enemy in counter-attacks. On 27th February the division was relieved by the Fifth Division, which included Count Gleichen's 15th Brigade from the Belfast District. After a rest the Fusiliers were back in the trenches, which they occupied the entire winter and spring, losing many officers and men, amongst them Major A. H. C. M'Gregor, Captain O. O'Hara, Lieutenant W. L. H. Hatch, Second-Lieutenant L. H. Coleman, and Major C. Conyers, who had gone temporarily to command the 1st Leinsters, was also killed. Lieut.-Col. P. R. Wood, who had taken the battalion to the front, received a brigade, and the personnel of the battalion ere the summer came had almost completely changed through the wastage of war. The 28th Division was destined for another theatre of war, and late in 1915 received orders to proceed to Salonika, in the region of which it spent some time. The Fusiliers went up country into Northern Macedonia in the middle of 1916, and served on the Struma Valley. Long marches and counter-marches through roadless country tried the troops severely, but by the second week of October, in common with the remainder of the troops in the valley they had crossed the river, and driven the Bulgars to their prepared positions on the other side. In the main attack of 30th October the Fusiliers distinguished themselves by aiding the up line of the strongly-fortified locality of Barakli Dzuma. A few weeks later they were transferred to the 31st Brigade of the Tenth Division to fill the vacancy caused by the amalgamation of the 5th and 6th Battalions of the same regiment, Lieut.Col. H. P. Orpen-Palmer being then the commanding officer. The subsequent operations of the brigade in Macedonia and Palestine are referred to in the account of the Tenth Division.

Reminiscent of the Old Days — Consolidating an Advanced Position.

Territorials, Special Reserve and Overseas

THE work of the Divisions named by no means exhausts the record of Ulstermen in the war. What of the hundreds who went to the Irish Guards, and from Landrecies down to the close of the war fought with that famous regiment, the 1st Battalion of which was commanded during part of the campaign by Lieut.-Col. R. C. A. M'Calmont, of East Antrim, now the regimental commander?

During the entire war the North Irish Horse kept up a steady stream of reinforcements to the front. Several squadrons went out with the B.E.F. in August, and early in the war a gallant officer of the corps fell in the person of Major Barry Combe, of Donacloney. The N.I.H. served in many capacities in various fields, but it was not until the majority were converted into infantry in 1916, and attached to the 9th R.I.F., that they had their bitterest fighting. How well they performed is told in the record of the Ulster Division. The Antrim Royal Garrison Artillery trained thousands of recruits at Kilroot and Grey Point during the war, despatching drafts to the front.

It would have been difficult to find a division of the army in any quarter of the globe in which North of Ireland men were not. They were especially plentiful in the ranks of the 1/6th Black Watch, a unit of the famous 51st Highland Division, for which the Germans had a most wholesome respect. Before the war this territorial battalion had its Belfast detachment, which crossed to Scotland every year for training. During the war their numbers expanded. Few of the original 6th Black Watch are now alive. A former N.C.O. of the battalion rose to command an Ulster division battalion during the war, while many others received commissions and decorations. The recruiting tour for the 1/4th Seaforth Highlanders in Belfast in 1915 gave several hundred men to that regiment, and they, too, proved amongst the finest soldiers in the 51st Division. Many other Ulstermen went to the London Irish, and a contingent from the postal service to the 8th Battalion London Regiment, the Post Office Rifles. The public schools battalions of the Royal Fusiliers attracted many Ulster boys, nearly all of whom laid down their lives, and the Church Lads' Battalion of the King's Royal Rifles likewise drew its North of Ireland recruits, several of whom won the D.C.M. Ulstermen in goodly numbers fought in the Bantam Battalions of the Royal Scots, the Cheshires, and the Sherwood Foresters, and in fact there was not a regiment of the army in which the Northern accent was not heard. The Cavalry, Artillery, Engineers, R.A.M.C., R.A.S.C., Labour Corps, and Machine-Gun Corps, found thousands of recruits in the Black North.

Mention should also be made of the work of the Special Reserve battalions of the three Ulster infantry regiments, which sent hundreds of drafts to the front. Newly-formed garrison battalions of the Royal Irish Rifles and Royal Irish Fusiliers in India, Egypt, and elsewhere played their part in the more hum-drum life of the soldier. They were largely made up of men no longer fit, through wounds or illness, for general service, and are still patiently awaiting the arrival of the regulars to relieve them. Towards the end of the war a new battalion of Inniskillings, the 13th (Service) Battalion came into being, and served in France, and also a new service battalion of the Royal Irish Fusiliers, designated the 11th Battalion.

The overseas troops, especially the Canadians, were alive with North of Ireland men, who volunteered in thousands in the Dominion. Two of them won the V.C. The Australians, New Zealanders and South Africans also had their full quota of Ulstermen, and when possible on leave they visited the old surroundings and the scenes of long ago.

The Women's Army

THE women of Ulster vied with their men folk in patriotic service. Short of taking a fighting part of their own, the women helped their country in every way open to them. Hundreds enlisted in the Queen Mary's Auxiliary Army Corps, serving at home and abroad, not a few experiencing the terrors of the incessant air raids upon Boulogne and other French towns. Many more went to the "Wrens," and other to the women's section of the Royal Air Force and to the Women's Legion. Not a few joint the R.A.S.C., and as motor drivers did yeoman service, but it was the nursing service that pre-eminently claimed the women. Sisters of Ulster abounded in all departments of the nursing force—in the Queen Alexandra's Imperial Military Nursing Service, in the V.A.D's, in the St. John Ambulance Association, and the various other organisations for the relief of the wounded and the sick. To some it was given to serve amid the perils of the casualty clearing stations, in constant danger of bombardment from air and land, and how heroically they stood the strain is shown by the records and the Military Medals awarded nurses from the North. Others did duty in the vast stationary hospitals along the French coast, from Calais to Etaples and inland to Rouen; others served in the home hospitals, and none more efficiently than those of the U.V.F. Hospital and its auxiliaries, the Royal Victoria Hospital, the Mater Hospital, and other institutions where the broken soldiers of the war were nursed back to health and strength. Hundreds of Ulster women worked throughout the war at munitions in Coventry and other centres, and also in the City of Belfast, while tens of thousands, in the quiet of their homes, worked incessantly for the men at the front. It is indeed impossible to realise how fully the activities of women sustained the civil fabric, but above all no one can ever estimate either the supreme value of the courage with which mothers and wives and lovers gave of their bravest and dearest to the State, or the marvellous patience and fortitude with which they endured the long agony of suspense, broken in too many cases by the receipt of the stunning news that the loved one had made the supreme sacrifice.

Ulstermen who won the V.C.

THE North of Ireland had its share of the Victoria Crosses awarded during the war, as the following record shows:—

34419 Sergt. DAVID NELSON, L. Battery Royal Horse Artillery.

For helping to bring the guns into action under heavy fire at Nery, on 1st September, 1914, and while severely wounded remaining with them until all the ammunition was expended, although he had been ordered to retire to cover.

Sergt. Nelson was a son of the late Mr. Geo. Nelson, Stranooden, Monaghan. He went to France as an N.C.O., and died of wounds there in April, 1918, when he was a Major.

1053 Private ROBERT MORROW, 1st Batt. Royal Irish Fusiliers.

For most conspicuous bravery near Messines, on 12th April, 1915, when he rescued and carried successively to places of comparative safety several men who had been buried in the debris of trenches wrecked by shell fire.

Private Morrow was the son of Mrs. Morrow, Newmills, Dungannon, and was killed in action a few months after winning the Cross.

1539 Colour-Sergeant FREDERICK WILLIAM HALL, 8th Canadian Battalion.

On 24th April, 1915, in the neighbourhood of Ypres, when a wounded man, who was lying some 15 yards from the trench, called for help, Company Sergeant-Major Hall endeavoured to reach him in the face of a very heavy enfilade fire which was being poured in by the enemy. Company Sergeant-Major Hall then made a second most gallant attempt, and was in the act of lifting up the wounded man to bring him in when he fell mortally wounded in the head.

This warrant officer belonged to Belfast, where his relatives still reside. He served in the Royal Inniskilling Fusiliers before emigrating to Canada.

10512 Sergeant JAMES SOMERS, 1st Battalion Royal Inniskilling Fusiliers (29th Division).

For most conspicuous bravery on the night of July 1-2, 1915, in the southern zone of the Gallipoli Peninsula, when, owing to hostile bombing, some of our troops had retired from a sap, Sergeant Somers remained alone on the spot until a party brought up bombs. He then climbed over into the Turkish trench and bombed the Turks with great effect. Later on he advanced into the open under heavy fire, and held back the enemy by throwing bombs into their flank until a barricade had been established. During this period he frequently ran to and from our trenches to obtain fresh supplies of bombs. By his gallantry and coolness Sergeant Somers was largely instrumental in effecting the recapture of a portion of our trench which had been lost.

Sergeant Somers was a native of Belturbet, Co. Cavan. He was gassed in France in 1917, and died at his parents' home, in Cloughjordan, on 7th May, 1918.

Captain JOHN A. SINTON, Indian Medical Service.

For most conspicuous bravery and devotion to duty at Orah Ruins, Mesopotamia, on the 21st January, 1916. Although shot through both arms and through the side he refused to go to hospital, and remained as long as daylight lasted attending to his duties under very heavy fire. In three previous actions Captain Sinton displayed the utmost bravery.

Capt. (now Lt. Col.) Sinton is a Lisburn man, and a graduate of Queen's University, Belfast. He is a son of Mrs. Sinton, Ulster Villas, Lisburn Road, Belfast.

Commander the Hon. EDWARD BARRY STEWART BINGHAM, R.N.

For the extremely gallant way in which he held his division in their attack, first on enemy destroyers and then on their battle-cruisers, in the Jutland Battle. He finally sighted the enemy battle-fleet, and, followed by the one remaining destroyer of his division ("Nicator"), with dauntless courage he closed to within 3,000 yards of the enemy in order to obtain a favourable position for firing the torpedoes. While making this attack, "Nestor" and "Nicator" were under concentrated fire of the secondary batteries of the High Sea Fleet. "Nestor" was subsequently sunk.

Commander Bingham is the third son of the fifth Baron Clanmorris, late of Bangor Castle, County Down. He was taken prisoner in the Jutland battle.

Lieutenant GEOFFREY ST. GEORGE SHILLINGTON CATHER, 9th Royal Irish Fusiliers (Ulster Division).

For most conspicuous bravery near Hamel, France, on 1st July, 1916. From 7 p.m. till midnight he searched "No Man's Land," and brought in three wounded men. Next morning, at 8 a.m., he continued his search, brought in another wounded man, and gave water to others, arranging for their rescue later. Finally, at 10-30 a.m., he took out water to another man, and was proceeding further on when he was himself killed. All this was carried out in full view of the enemy, and under direct machine gun fire and intermittent artillery fire. He set a splendid example of courage and self-sacrifice.

Lieut. Cather was a son of the late Mr. R. G. Cather and Mrs. Cather, and grandson of the late Mr. Thos. Shillington, J.P., Tavanagh House, Portadown and Rev. Robert Cather, Belfast. He was 25 years of age.

14/18278 Private WILLIAM FREDERICK M'FADZEAN, 14th Batt. Royal Irish Rifles (Ulster Division).

For most conspicuous bravery near Thiepval Wood, on 1st July, 1916. While in a concentration trench, and opening a box of bombs for distribution prior to an attack, the box slipped down into the trench, which was crowded with men, and two of the safety pins fell out. Private M'Fadzean, instantly realising the danger to his comrades, with heroic courage threw himself on the top of the bombs. The bombs exploded, blowing him to pieces, but only one other man was injured. He well knew his danger, being himself a bomber, but without a moment's hesitation he gave his life for his comrades.

Private M'Fadzean was a son of Mr. William M'Fadzean, Rubicon, Cregagh, Belfast, and was born in Lurgan, in 1895. He was on the staff of Messrs. Spence, Bryson & Co., Belfast, before joining the colours.

12/18645 Private ROBERT QUIGG, 12th Batt. Royal Irish Rifles (Ulster Division.)

For most conspicuous bravery, Hamel, France, on 1st July, 1916. He advanced to the assault with his platoon three times. Early next morning, hearing a rumour that his platoon officer was lying out wounded, he went out seven times to look for him under heavy shell and machine gun fire, each time bringing back a wounded man. The last man he dragged in on a waterproof sheet from within a few yards of the enemy's wire. He was seven hours engaged in this most gallant work, and finally was so exhausted that he had to give it up.

Private Quigg (now a sergeant) is a son of Mr. Robert Quigg, Carnkirk, Bushmills, a guide at the Giant's Causeway. He was born in 1885, and enlisted from the U.V.F. at Ballymoney. The officer whom he tried to save was the late Sir Harry Macnaghten, Bart., of Dundarave, Bushmills.

Captain ERIC NORMAN FRANKLAND BELL, 9th Batt. Royal Inniskilling Fusiliers (Ulster Division).

For most conspicuous bravery at Thiepval, on 1st July, 1916. He was in command of a trench mortar battery, and advanced with the infantry to the attack. When our front line was hung up by enfilading machine gun fire, Captain Bell crept forward and shot the machine gunner. Later on, no less than three occasions, when our bombing parties, which were clearing the enemies' trenches, were unable to advance, he went forward alone and threw trench mortar bombs among the enemy. When he had no more bombs available he stood on the parapet, under intense fire, and used a rifle with great coolness and effect on the enemy advancing to counter-attack. Finally he was killed rallying and reorganising infantry parties which had lost their officers. All this was outside the scope of his

V.C.s OF FOUR CAMPAIGNS

normal duties with his battery. He gave his life in his supreme devotion to duty.

Capt. Bell was a son of the late Capt. E. H. Bell, who was Quartermaster at the Inniskillings' Depot in Omagh. His mother is an Enniskillen lady, residing at Bootle.

3/5027 Private THOMAS HUGHES, 6th Batt. Connaught Rangers (Sixteenth Division).

For most conspicuous bravery and determination at Guillemont, France, on the 3rd Sept., 1916. He was wounded in an attack, but returned at once to the firing line after having his wounds dressed. Later, seeing a hostile machine-gun, he dashed out in front of his company, shot the gunner, and, single-handed, captured the gun. Though again wounded he brought back three or four prisoners.

Private Hughes is a Castleblayney man, and was employed at the Curragh before enlisting.

Second-Lieut. JOHN SPENCER DUNVILLE, 1st Royal Dragoons.

For most conspicuous bravery near Epehy, France, on 24th and 25th June, 1917. When in charge of a party consisting of scouts and Royal Engineers engaged in the demolition of the enemy's wire, this officer displayed great gallantry and disregard of all personal danger. In order to ensure the absolute success of the work entrusted to him, 2nd Lieut. Dunville placed himself between an N.C.O. of the Royal Engineers and the enemy's fire, and, thus protected, this N.C.O. was enabled to complete a work of great importance. 2nd Lieut. Dunville, although severely wounded, continued to direct his men in the wire cutting and general operations until the raid was successfully completed, thereby setting a magnificent example of courage, determination, and devotion to duty, to all ranks under his command. The gallant officer has since succumbed to his wounds.

Second-Lieutenant Dunville was a son of Mr. John Dunville, Redburn, Holywood. He was 21 years of age when he was killed.

Second-Lieutenant JAS. SAMUEL EMERSON, 9th Royal Inniskilling Fusiliers (Ulster Division).

For repeated acts of most conspicuous bravery N. of La Vacquerie on 6th December, 1917. He led the company in an attack and cleared 400 yards of trench, though wounded, when the enemy attacked in superior numbers, he sprang out of the trench with eight men and met the attack in the open, killing many and taking six prisoners. For three hours after this, all other officers having been casualties, he remained with his company, refusing to go to the dressing station and repeatedly repelled bombing attacks. Later, when the enemy again attacked in superior numbers, he led his men to repel the attack, and was mortally wounded. His heroism, when worn out and exhausted from loss of blood, inspired his men to hold out, though almost surrounded, till reinforcements arrived and dislodged the enemy.

Second-Lieut. Emerson, who was 22 years of age, was a son of the late Mr. John Emerson, of Collon, and brother of Mr. W. Emerson, Armagh. He was for a time in the 9th Royal Irish Rifles (West Belfast Volunteers) before receiving a commission.

681886 Sergt. CYRIL EDWARD GOURLEY, M.M., Royal Field Artillery.

For most conspicuous bravery when in command of a section of howitzers, at Little Priel Farm, east of Epehy, France, on 30th November, 1917. Though the enemy advanced in force, getting within 400 yards in front, between 300 to 400 yards to one flank, and with snipers in rear, Sergt. Gourley managed to keep one gun in action practically throughout the day. Though frequently driven off he always returned, carrying ammunition, laying and firing the gun himself, taking first one and then another of the detachment to assist him. When the enemy advanced he pulled his gun out of the pit and engaged a machine-gun at 500 yards, knocking it out with a direct hit. All day he held the enemy in check, firing with open sights on enemy parties in full view at 300 to 800 yards, and thereby saved his guns, which were withdrawn at nightfall. He had previously been awarded the Military Medal for conspicuous gallantry.

Sergt. Gourley is a son of Mr. J. Gourley, late of Galbally, Dromore, Co. Tyrone, and now of Liverpool.

75361 Company Sgt.-Major ROBERT HANNA, Canadian Infantry.

For most conspicuous bravery at Lens, France, on 21st September, 1917, when his company met with most severe enemy resistance and all the company officers became casualties. A strong point, heavily protected by wire and held by a machine gun, had beaten off three assaults of the company with heavy casualties. This warrant officer, under heavy machine-gun and rifle fire, cooly [sic] collected a party of men, and, leading them against the strong point, rushed through the wire and personally bayoneted three of the enemy and brained the fourth, capturing the position and silencing the machine-gun. This most courageous action displayed courage and personal bravery of the highest order at this most critical moment of the attack, was responsible for the capture of a most important tactical point, and but for his daring action and determined handling of a desperate situation the attack would not have succeeded. Company Sergt.-Major Hanna's outstanding gallantry, personal courage, and determined leading of his company is deserving of the highest possible reward.

This gallant warrant officer (now a lieutenant) is a son of Mr. Robert Hill Hanna, farmer, of Aughnahoory, Kilkeel, Co. Down. He was born in that place, and emigrated to Canada in 1902.

6/17978 Private JAMES DUFFY, 6th Battalion Royal Inniskilling Fusiliers (10th Division).

For most conspicuous bravery at Lerlina Peak, Palestine, on 27th December, 1917, displayed whilst his company was holding a very exposed position. Private Duffy (a stretcher-bearer) and another stretcher-bearer went out to bring in a seriously wounded comrade; when the other stretcher-bearer was wounded he returned to get another man; when again going forward the relief stretcher-bearer was killed. Private Duffy then went forward alone, and, under heavy fire, succeeded in getting both wounded men under cover and attended to their injuries. His gallantry undoubtedly saved both men's lives, and he showed throughout an utter disregard of danger under very heavy fire.

Private Duffy is a son of the late Mr. Peter Duffy, Bonagee, Letterkenny, County Donegal, and is 26 years of age.

Second-Lieutenant EDMUND DE WIND, 15th Battalion Royal Irish Rifles (Ulster Division).

For most conspicuous bravery and self-sacrifice on 21st March, 1918, at the Racecourse Redoubt, near Groagie. For seven hours he held this important post, and though twice wounded and practically single-handed he maintained his position until another section could be got to his help. On two occasions, with two N.C.O.'s only, he got out on top under heavy machine-gun and rifle fire and cleared the enemy out of the trench, killing many. He continued to repel attack after attack until he was mortally wounded and collapsed. His valour, self-sacrifice, and example were of the highest order.

Second-Lieut. De Wind was youngest son of the late Mr. A. H. De Wind, C.E., Belfast, and of Mrs. de Wind, who now resides at Kinvara, Comber. He was born in 1883, and was a bank clerk in Cavan before going to Canada, whence he returned to enlist.

Lieut.-Colonel RICHARD ANNESLEY WEST, D.S.O., M.C., North Irish Horse, attached Tank Corps.

For most conspicuous bravery, leadership, and self-sacrifice at Courcelles and Vaulx, Vraacourt, France, on 21st August, 1918, and 2nd September, 1918. During an attack the infantry having lost their bearings, in the dense fog, this officer at once collected and reorganised any men he could find, and led them to their objective in face of a heavy machine-gun fire. Throughout the whole action he displayed the most utter disregard of danger, and the capture of the objective was in a great part due to his initiative and gallantry. On a subsequent occasion it was intended that a battalion of light tanks under the command of this officer should exploit the initial infantry and heavy tank attack. He therefore went forward in order to keep in touch with the progress of the battle, and arrived at the front line when the enemy were in process of delivering a local counter-attack. The infantry battalion had suffered heavy officer casualties, and its flanks were exposed. Realising that there was a danger of the battalion giving way, he at once rode out in front of them under extremely heavy machine-gun and rifle fire, and rallied the men. In spite of the fact that the enemy were close upon him he took charge of the situation and detailed non-commissioned officers to replace officer casualties. He then rode up and down in front of them in face of certain death, encouraging the men and calling to them, "Stick it, men; show them fight; and for God's sake put up a good fight." He fell riddled by machine-gun bullets. The magnificent bravery of this very gallant officer at the critical moment inspired the infantry to redoubled efforts, and the hostile attack was defeated.

Lieut.-Colonel West was the youngest son of Mr. Augustus George West, of White Park, County Fermanagh, and had a most gallant career in the war. He was 39 years of age.

The following V.C.'s were awarded to Ulster units, the recipients not being Ulstermen:—

Capt. GERALD ROBERT O'SULLIVAN, 1st Batt. Royal Inniskilling Fusiliers (since killed in action).—

Four Ulster Division Heroes who won the V.C. and lost their lives.

Capt. E. N. F. BELL, 9th Batt. Royal Inniskilling Fusiliers (Tyrone Volunteers), Killed 1st July, 1916.

2nd Lieut. J. S. EMERSON, 9th Batt. Royal Inniskilling Fusiliers (Tyrone Volunteers), Killed 6th Dec., 1917.

Lieut. G. St. G. S. CATHER, 9th Batt. Royal Irish Fusiliers (Armagh, Monaghan and Cavan Volunteers), Killed 1st July, 1916.

Private WM. M'FADZEAN, 14th Royal Irish Rifles (Young Citizen Volunteers of Belfast), Killed 1st July, 1916.

S.W. of Krithia, Gallipoli, on the night of 1st-2nd July, 1915. (29th Division.)

Lieut.-Col. J. SHERWOOD-KELLY, C.M.G., D.S.O., Norfolk Regiment, Commanding 1st Batt. Royal Inniskilling Fusiliers.—At Marcoing, France, on 20th November, 1917. (29th Division.)

Second-Lieut. C. L. KNOX, 150th Field Co. Royal Engineers (Ulster Division), at Tugny, France, on 22nd March, 1918.

42364 Lance-Corpl. ERNEST SEAMAN, 2nd Batt. Royal Inniskilling Fusiliers (since killed in action).— At Terbond, France, on 29th September, 1918. (Ulster Division.)

42954 Private NORMAN HARVEY, 1st Batt. Royal Inniskilling Fusiliers (Ulster Division).—At Ingoyten, on 25th October, 1918.

Numerous other V.C.'s were won by officers and men of Ulster parentage, but who themselves were not natives of the province. Amongst these were the late Lieut. James Anson Otho Brooke, 2nd Batt. Gordon Highlanders (Aberdeen), who was one of the Brookes of Brookeborough. He gained the Cross at Gheluvelt, on 29th October, 1914, and lost his life on the same day. 11213 Sergt. R. Downie, 2nd Batt. Royal Dublin Fusiliers who was awarded the cross for his bravery in attack on gunposts last year, Les Boeufs, France, on 25th October,

1916, was the son of Laurencetown (Co. Down) parents and was born in Glasgow, where the family have lived for nearly forty years.

The late Flight Sub-Lieut. R. A. J. Warneford, who destroyed the first Zeppelin, on 7th June, 1915, was a grandson of the late Mr. Alexander Campbell. C.I.E., D.S.O., Ballyalton, Co. Down.

Ulster and the Navy

FIGHTING AND BUILDING

DURING the War thousands of Ulstermen served in the Royal Navy, the Royal Naval Reserve, and the Royal Naval Volunteer Reserve, and the Royal Fleet Reserve. From the mighty super-dreadnought to the humblest minesweeper or motor patrol boat there was scarcely a ship without its quota of North of Ireland men and there was scarcely a naval loss in the war that did not bring sorrow to some Ulster home. This was notably the case in connection with the sinking of the Cruiser "Hawke" in the North Sea, in 1915, over fifty Belfastmen going down with that ship. In the Jutland Battle which gave Commander the Hon. E. B. S. Bingham the V.C., Ulstermen fought and fell, while isolated disasters like the blowing up of the "Formidable" and the "Natal" cost the lives of many more. When Lord Kitchener went down with the "Hampshire" several North of Ireland men, including the ship's surgeon, perished with him. And so it was all through. It was the same in the Mercantile Marine, which was virtually a branch of the Admiralty. Ship after ship was torpedoed, but that did not daunt the spirit of the sailors. Companies like the Head Line had numerous vessels sent to the bottom but the survivors never failed to turn up for another boat.

Belfast's greatest work for the Navy was done in the shipyards of Messrs. Harland & Wolff, Ltd. and Workman, Clark & Co., Ltd.

Immediately after the declaration of War steps were taken to adapt the Queen's Island plant to the new conditions required for the execution of Admiralty contracts. The first important work taken in hand was the transforming of a number of cargo and other boats into vessels bearing a very close resemblance to battleships. The idea was to mislead the enemy regarding the strength of the British Fleet and the identity of particular ships. The phantom vessels were rigged exactly like cruisers and battleships, but in reality they were no more than imitations. They carried wooden guns, and ostensibly, they had all the equipment of the formidable vessels they were intended to represent. For fighting purposes they were, of course, worthless; but the deception could only be discovered on very close investigation, and in striking terror into the hearts of the enemy they were almost as potent as vessels armed with big guns of the latest type. One of them stood off New York for a considerable time, intimidating a big German cruiser, which was afraid to leave the harbour while the "dummy" ship had it under observation. Another was sunk at the Dardanelles. The "dummy" ships were ubiquitous, and if they were so inclined the crews could tell many amusing stories of the desperate efforts which huge German battleships made to avoid them out of sheer terror. The crews ran very serious risks in deliberately running across the path of armed enemy vessels, because if the latter had opened fire on them they could not possibly have replied. To travel on a "dummy" was a great adventure and a grave peril, but no difficulty whatever was experienced in obtaining crews. The phantom ships numbered fourteen and were called after notable vessels fighting in the Navy List; they included the "St. Vincent," "Collingwood," "Iron Duke," "King George the Fifth," "Centurion," "Orion," "Marlborough," "Audacious," "Ajax," "Vanguard," "Invincible," "Queen Mary," "Indomitable" and "Tiger." After they had served their object as "bogey men" they were converted into cargo and oil-carriers, and one was utilised as a balloon ship. It was in connection with the preparation of the "dummy" ships that dilution of labour was first agreed to at the Queen's Island. The men consented to this departure because of their desire to help their country at a very critical period. While at sea the "dummies" were formed into a cruiser squadron, with Captain Haddock, of "Olympic" fame, as the Commodore.

After the "dummies" had been sent to sea, Harland & Wolff turned their attention to the building of monitors, a number of which, were employed off the Belgian coast with very satisfactory results. They were designed on a plan which gave them special protection against torpedo attacks, and they were armed with powerful guns. The protection was derived from an ingenious contrivance of the "bulges" which gave the vessels a greater resisting power than that possessed by any other type of ship. The monitors were by no means remarkable for grace and symmetry of line, but they were exceedingly useful owing to the character of their armament and their light draught. The idea of employing them on the Belgian coast originated with Lord Fisher, who was at that time the First Sea Lord, and Mr. Winston Churchill, then First Lord of the Admiralty, facilitated their completion by expediting the delivery of the guns. The first of the monitors was completed in 4½ months. The workmen displayed keen interest in their construction and deserve great credit for the energy and enthusiasm with which they performed their labours. The monitors built in Belfast were named "Abercrombie," "Havelock," "Lord Clive," "General Craufurd," "Earl of Peterborough," "Sir Thomas Picton" and "Terror."

Messrs. Harland & Wolff also built five river boats—called "Whippets"—for use in the East. These craft drew a small draught, and were fitted with guns.

The "Glorious," a fast cruiser is a production of Queen's Island. At the time she was launched she was the most powerful ship in the United Kingdom, and she set up a new record in her speed trials. The "Vindictive" (first named the "Cavendish"), another fast cruiser, was also built at Queen's Island. Both the "Glorious" and the "Vindictive" won distinction in the War.

On the engineering side the war produced some notable developments at the Queen's Island. It was here that the "Curacoa," Sir Reginald Tyrhitt's flagship was engined, and the engines for several submarines of the largest type were also supplied by Messrs. Harland & Wolff. The firm had never previously built submarine engines, but the plant was quickly adapted to the purpose.

Messrs. Harland & Wolff also did a vast amount of repair work, and have also converted into cruisers and hospital ships a number of vessels which were originally intended for cargo and passengers. Many of the large liners that were on the stocks when war broke out were promptly transferred into armed cruisers. The White Star liners "Britannic" and the "Olympic" were both converted into hospital ships.

The firm have launched to date, upwards of a quarter of a million tons of standard ships ordered by the Government in a time of national emergency. The Belfast Yards hold the record for rapidity in turning out standard ships.

Messrs. Workman, Clark & Co.

MESSRS. Workman, Clark & Co's. work for the nation during the War was both vast and varied. During the War period they handled 1396 ships of various types, either in the way of building, repairing, or overhauling. These vessels ranged from the largest battle cruisers down to nimble patrol boats, and from stately liners to barrage and bomb defence vessels.

Once the slips had been cleared of merchant tonnage the firm was engaged practically solely in work for the Admiralty, and the variety of the types of vessels dealt with is a tribute both to the resources and workmanship of the staff. A multitude of craft of the most varied kinds was either constructed or repaired, but notwithstanding the strain thrown on the concern orders were got through with a despatch creditable to the patriotism of the workers and adding fresh lustre to the laurels of Belfast as a shipbuilding port.

The first large commission for the Admiralty was the alteration of four of the older type of cruisers, the "Endymion," "Theseus," "Edgar," and "Grafton" in such a manner as to make them fulfil the purpose of monitors. This was done by building on to the sides of the vessels protective projections so as to give considerably more displacement and also to protect them from torpedo attack. These projections ran almost the entire length of the vessels, and were done in dry dock in record time, the work being carried on continuously night and day. This was so successfully carried out that the firm was asked to undertake the task of fitting portable projections on the battleship "Revenge." This entailed the building of the projections in sections at the yard, the sections being afterwards fitted on the vessel afloat. It also necessitated very accurate workmanship, and the Admiralty expressed themselves as well satisfied with the manner in which it had been accomplished.

To enumerate the naval refits and repair jobs carried out would be too lengthy a task. Amongst the more notable vessels of H.M. Fleet thus dealt with were the famous battle-cruiser "Invincible," the battleships "Africa," "Albermarle," "Britannia," "Commonwealth," "Revenge," and the "Russell," the cruisers "Cochrane," "Cumberland," and "Hampshire," the light cruisers "Circe," "Fearless," and "Adventure"; also torpedo destroyers, submarines, patrol vessels, and mine-sweepers in continuous succession.

As a matter of fact, taking the work done in all the docks, Messrs. Workman, Clark, & Co., Ltd., handled an average of almost one vessel per day during the war period. The repairs and overhauls to naval craft meant the incessant utilisation of the dry docks of the port, and never was the foresight of the Harbour Commissioners in providing the large docks on the County Down side of the river more fully justified than during this period.

The record of the firm in the way of new construction was also full of variety and almost fascinating in its scope. To begin with, two small monitors were built fitted with 6 in. guns, and these vessels were launched and fitted out for sea within eight weeks from the day of the laying of the keel. Then seven of the celebrated high-speed "Q" boats were constructed at intervals, and a number of heavily-armed sloops were also built. Following them a large number of barges and pontoons for special purposes of the Admiralty were completed in a very brief period.

The first oil tank steamer, "Texol," was constructed, this vessel having a deadweight capacity of almost 7,000 tons, and a speed of 15 knots at sea.

The next work to be tackled was a series of stern wheel hospital ships for the River Tigris, four of these being constructed. One was completely finished and went out under her own steam to her far-off destination, the other three being sent out to the East for re-erection. These vessels were specially equipped with every hospital convenience, and have been found very suitable for their purpose.

The next craft of a special type to be constructed were ten barrage vessels and six boom defence vessels. The barrage vessels were each fitted with four powerful searchlights, and were suitable for putting up a barrage of light wherever desired. They were also fitted with guns for protection. The boom defence vessels were intended for carrying the boom nets, and were also fitted with guns and special hauling winches for raising and lowering the nets as desired.

In addition to this work, three large boats were altered from their original design as cargo boats, and fitted with large circular tanks, in which oil could be carried in bulk. These tanks were the full width of the ship, and extended from the tank top to the upper deck. An immense amount of work was involved in carrying out these changes, and the vessels have proved very successful. At this particular time oil tank vessels were very scarce, and these three large vessels were each able to carry a cargo of about 10,000 tons of oil.

The "Sandhurst," a torpedo boat destroyer depot ship, was a most interesting ship. Originally a cargo boat, she was converted into a depot ship, and the fit-up for this purpose involved the erection on board of fitting shops, moulding shops, foundry, smithy, and various other shops, so that any repairs of any reasonable kind could be carried out on the destroyers without them having to return to port.

A number of steamers were fitted out as hospital ships. These included the "Panama," "Essequibo," and the "Formosa," while quite a host of vessels were fitted out as troopships. Several liners were fitted as auxiliary cruisers, the "Coronado," "Mantua," "Patia," and "Patuca" being examples of this class of work.

While the work in connection with the re-fitting of destroyers, sloops, battleships, cruisers, etc., was going on, the new construction for the Admiralty was partially suspended in favour of standard ships. Some of these vessels have been turned out in very quick time. During their construction one of the firm's men established a new world's riveting record in the north yard, the south yard and engine works replying by making a record in the way of finishing a standard ship, an 8,000 ton vessel being completed in 3¾ days from the time of the launch.

The engine works erected the boilers and engines in all the vessels built in the shipyard, and in addition carried out an enormous quantity of repair work and overhaul work to engines and boilers of almost every kind of craft in the Navy.

They also carried out a large amount of work for the Ministry of Munitions in the making of 9.2-inch and 6-inch shells, a very large number of these being turned out; also trench mortars and hand grenades.

Much valuable work for the Navy was done during the war by the North of Ireland Shipbuilding Co., Ltd., Londonderry, and the Larne Shipbuilding Co., while the Messrs. J. & R. Thompson, Ltd., and M'Laughlin & Harvey, Ltd., Belfast, opened a joint shipyard at Warrenpoint, where they built ferro-concrete ships to the order of the Board of Admiralty.

Ulster and the Air Force

THE attractions of flying proved irresistible to the youth of Ulster, many of whom joined the Royal Naval Air Service and the Royal Flying Corps, now merged in the Royal Air Force. In the recruiting boom of 1918 this force was the great magnet for the majority of the lads who joined from the North in various capacities.

The exploits of the Ulster airmen would fill a volume. Many of them made the supreme sacrifice, but the memory of their deeds and personalities remain with us.

The brothers Tyrrell and the brothers Cowan are but two of the noble band who fell in foreign lands. There are others known to all, of whom the late Leslie Porter was perhaps the outstanding figure, and of those who survived the perils of air and foe none have a finer record than Flight-Lieut. Dickey, of Londonderry, who fought Zepps. and submarines, and carried out bombardments on land and sea that won for him practically every decoration open to airmen save the Victoria Cross.

The part Ulster played in the development of the Air Force cannot be overestimated, because 95 per cent. of the linen for Britain's wonderful aeroplanes was manufactured in our mills and factories. Almost the entire linen industry was engaged in this work, and the output ran into millions of yards. And not only that, but Messrs. Harland & Wolff with characteristic enterprise established an aeroplane factory wherein was built the largest class of aeroplane, the firm doing everything that was necessary in the production of the machine except build the engines. They also constructed an aerodrome at Aldergrove, near Crumlin, where they had an area of 500 acres.

Greetings

The record of the Thirty-sixth Division will ever be the pride of Ulster. At Thiepval in the great battle of the Somme on July 1st, 1916; at Wytschaete on June 17th, 1917, in the storming of the Messines Ridge; on the Canal du Nord in the attack on the Hindenburg Line of November 20th in the same year; on March 21st, 1918, near Fontaine-les-Clercs, defending their positions long after they were isolated and surrounded by the enemy; and later in the month at Andechy in the days of "backs to the wall," they acquired a reputation for conduct and devotion deathless in the military history of the United Kingdom, and repeatedly signalised in the despatches of the Commander-in-Chief.

These Celebrations of Victory, and of Peace following upon Victory, commemorate and proclaim to future generations their country's gratitude to the living and the dead.

WINSTON S. CHURCHILL,
Secretary of State for War.

PEACE CELEBRATIONS.

PRESENTED on behalf of the Citizens of Belfast by the Citizens' Committee to the Ulster Service Men, as a Souvenir of Peace Day.

J. C. WHITE, Lord Mayor,
Hon. Treasurer.

R. I. CALWELL,
HERBERT DIXON,
W. GIBSON, M.D.,
T. E. McCONNELL,
F. W. MONEYPENNY,
S. BLACKER QUIN,
J. W. STOREY,

Hon. Secretaries.

CITY HALL,
BELFAST,
Saturday, 9th August, 1919